Gifts from the
KITCHEN

Gifts from the KITCHEN

PAMELA WESTLAND

MADE FOR GIVING

Reader's Digest

PUBLISHED BY THE READER'S DIGEST ASSOCIATION LIMITED
LONDON · NEW YORK · SYDNEY · CAPE TOWN · MONTREAL

A READER'S DIGEST BOOK

Published by The Reader's Digest Association Limited
Berkeley Square House
Berkeley Square
London W1X 6AB

Conceived, edited and designed by Marshall Editions
170 Piccadilly, London W1V 9DD

Copyright © 1997 by Marshall Editions Developments Limited

ISBN 0-276-42305-4

A CIP catalogue for this book is available from the British Library

Reader's Digest®, The Digest and the Pegasus logo are registered
trademarks of The Reader's Digest Association, Inc., of Pleasantville,
New York, USA.

Printed and bound in Italy

EDITOR LINDSAY MCTEAGUE
ART EDITOR KATHERINE HARKNESS
PHOTOGRAPHER CHRISTINE HANSCOMB
FOOD STYLISTS BRIDGET SARGESON, LINDA MACLEAN
HAND MODEL MICHAELA MOHER
COPY EDITORS JOLIKA FESZT, BEVERLY LEBLANC,
MAGGI MCCORMICK
DTP EDITORS LESLEY GILBERT, KATE WAGHORN
PRODUCTION EDITOR EMMA DIXON
EDITORIAL DIRECTOR SOPHIE COLLINS
ART DIRECTOR SEAN KEOGH
PRODUCTION ROBERT K. CHRISTIE, NIKKI INGRAM

Contents

INTRODUCTION

THERE IS SOMETHING IMMENSELY SATISFYING in handing over an elegant parcel or box to your host at a party and hearing the thrilled exclamation, 'You made this all yourself!'

Creating a lively, innovative wrapping for a gift is as important for the end impression as what's inside the parcel: your present should look good and taste marvellous. With a little know-how, it is not hard to do.

This book gives comprehensive instructions on both making and packaging, so that your gift has the right blend of the personal touch and the professional finish. All the projects are attainable; even a novice will be rewarded with excellent results. And as your confidence grows, you will find it easy to mix and match the recipes and packaging ideas to create any number of variations. If you're timid about your crafting skills, try the simple fabric wrapping for a Christmas cake on pages 122–23; it couldn't be easier to achieve. And if it's cooking that makes you nervous, start with the Chocolate Rum Truffles on pages 62–63; the delicious end results belie the easy-to-follow recipe.

You can make your own containers – boxes, bags or paper cones – or buy simple ones to decorate yourself, such as wooden or woven baskets, flowerpots or pencil holders. The finish on the gifts here is accomplished without having to resort to expensive or elaborate fixings – silver sweet wrappers, a few pressed leaves or a handful of shells gathered on the beach can be made into decorative trimming for any number of simple and delicious things to eat. Above all, enjoy being creative as you perfect the art of giving.

Always follow one set of measurements – either metric or imperial – all the way through a recipe or project. Many of the recipes make more than you will need to fill the package – this is so you can choose the best ones to give as gifts. ✲

MAKING A SQUARE BOX

Once you have learned how to make a simple square box, you can adjust the measurements and vary the materials you use to create a satisfying variety of packages.

YOU WILL NEED

Cutting mat, craft knife, ruler, pencil, scissors

Piece of medium-weight cardboard twice as long as it is wide (see sizing guide below)

Double-sided tape, 5 cm (2 in) wide

SIZING BOX BASE & LID

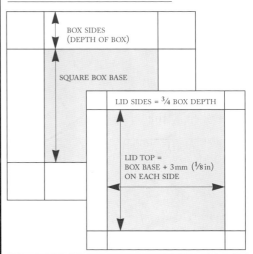

BOX SIDES (DEPTH OF BOX)

SQUARE BOX BASE

LID SIDES = ¾ BOX DEPTH

LID TOP = BOX BASE + 3mm (⅛ in) ON EACH SIDE

Note

For a rectangular box use the basic principles outlined above but make the base a rectangle. You can make your box of coloured card or cover it in patterned paper (for instructions see pages 114–15, steps 2–7).

TO MAKE A SQUARE BOX *15 x 15 x 4.5 cm (6 x 6 x 1¾ in)*

1 Place a piece of card 25 by 50 cm (10 by 20 in) on the cutting mat. Measure, draw and cut a square 24 by 24 cm (9½ by 9½ in) to form the base and sides of the box. Measure and draw a line 4.5 cm (1¾ in) in from and parallel to each side. This measurement is the depth of the box. The square in the centre, between the four lines, is the base.

2 With a craft knife, score along all the pencil lines, but do not cut through the cardboard at this stage. To make the flaps that will form square corners, cut through one of the two pencil lines at each corner.

3 Measure and cut strips of double-sided tape to cover each of the squares at the corners. With the scored side of the cardboard still uppermost, stick the tape on to each corner.

4 Turn the cardboard over so the scored side is on the mat. Crease along all the scored lines and bring up the sides to form the depth of the box.

5 Peel off the backing from the tape at each corner in turn. With the sticky side inside, overlap the cut section and the side of the box and press the two thicknesses of cardboard together to give neat, square corners.

6 To make the box lid, measure, draw and cut a square 22 by 22 cm (8¾ by 8¾ in) from the remaining cardboard. Measure and draw a line 2.75 cm (1¼ in) in from and parallel to each of the four sides. This represents the side of the lid. Repeat steps 2 to 7 to finish the lid. ✤

EQUIPMENT

PENCIL, RULER, SCISSORS, CUTTING MAT, craft knife and double-sided tape are all you need to make most of the packages here. And some of them don't even require this much equipment.

You may already have many of these items at home, but if not, a visit to a craft shop will ensure that you return home with all the tools of the trade. Cardboard in different colours, prettily or strikingly patterned wrapping paper, paints, stencils, ribbons and bows – all will transform a plain parcel into a masterpiece.

Add a finishing touch of a tassel handle, a bunch of crystallised roses or a personalised embossed gift tag. And with the projects here to inspire you, you can let your imagination run riot and make gifts to suit any number of your friends.

MAKING A ROUND BOX

A round box and lid is made of four pieces of cardboard – two circles and two thinner strips.

YOU WILL NEED

Cutting mat, craft knife, ruler, pencil, scissors

Piece of medium-weight cardboard for box base and top of lid (see Note below)

Piece of thinner cardboard for sides (see Note below)

Pair of compasses (or you can use a plate or other round item as a guide)

Parcel tape, 5 cm (2 in) wide

Sheet of wrapping paper (see Note below)

Double-sided tape, 5 cm (2 in) wide

SIZING BOX BASE & LID   SIDES

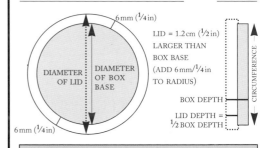

6 mm (¼ in)

LID = 1.2 cm (½ in) LARGER THAN BOX BASE (ADD 6 mm/¼ in TO RADIUS)

DIAMETER OF LID

DIAMETER OF BOX BASE

CIRCUMFERENCE

BOX DEPTH

LID DEPTH = ½ BOX DEPTH

6 mm (¼ in)

Note

Calculate how much you will need: Medium-weight cardboard Width is equal to one diameter plus 2.5 cm (1 in); its length is twice the width. Thinner cardboard Length is equal to the circumference of the lid; its width is the sum of the box and lid sides. Wrapping paper Length is same as thinner cardboard; width is width of both pieces of cardboard plus 5 cm (2 in) for overlap.

— 8 —

TO MAKE A ROUND BOX *18 cm (7 in) in diameter and 5 cm (2 in) deep*

1 Place a piece of medium-weight cardboard 20 by 40 cm (8 by 16 in) on the cutting mat. For the box base, draw a circle 18 cm (7 in) wide, using compasses or a round item as a guide. With the craft knife, cut out the circle. For the lid, draw and cut out a circle 19 cm (7½ in) in diameter.

2 From a piece of thinner cardboard 8 by 60 cm (3 by 24 in), draw and cut a strip to make the side of the box. It should be 5 by 58 cm (2 by 23 in). This is the depth of the box by the circumference plus 2.5 cm (1 in) for overlap. For the side of the lid cut a strip 2 by 58 cm (1 by 23 in).

3 To make the box base, cut about 36 strips of parcel tape 1.5 cm (½ in) long and stick the ends around the rim of a bowl so they are at hand. With the cardboard circle in your hand, stick the strips of tape close together around the circumference, so half of each strip overhangs the edge of the circle.

4 Place the cardboard circle on the work surface so the sticky side of the tape is uppermost. Place the strip for the side of the box upright against the edge of the circle and, starting at one end of the strip, bend over and stick the strips of parcel tape to join the two pieces.

5 When you reach the other end of the cardboard strip, cut it so that the two ends butt up evenly, then cover the join with a strip of parcel tape. Make the lid in the same way as the box, following steps 3 and 4.

6 To cover the box with wrapping paper, follow the instructions on pages 118–19, steps 1–7. You will need a piece of paper about 30 by 60 cm (12 by 24 in). ✷

Small Treats

✤ THE WARM, HOMELY SMELL OF baking is implicit in our selection of biscuits, and there is an irresistible diversity of recipes, ranging from traditional Scottish shortbread to chequerboard vanilla and peppermint biscuits. Add a touch of spice with cinnamon and nut bars, gingerbread people, or ginger and honey fairings sparkling with edible gold leaf, or for a tropical taste try coconut wreath biscuits or lemon sugar-crystal buns. Spell out the recipient's name with alphabet biscuits for a more personal gift, and try cheese shells packed with sun-dried tomatoes for a savoury snack.

There is just as much variety in the packaging ideas too. You can learn how to make cut and folded cardboard boxes, a ribbon-weave panel for a box, a gingham pouch and a mini carrier bag. You can try your hand at painting and stencilling or stamping ready-made boxes and baskets, or turning some wire and a few trimmings into a glitzy package.

Scottish Shortbread

As traditionally Scottish as its tartan wrappings, this shortbread can be served with morning coffee, a cup of tea, or to accompany a rich and creamy dessert.

RECIPE INGREDIENTS

250 g (8 oz) cold unsalted butter, cut into small pieces

250 g (8 oz) plain flour

125 g (4 oz) caster sugar

125 g (4 oz) fine semolina

2 teaspoons (10 ml) vanilla essence

Makes 18 biscuits, enough to fill 3 boxes

PACKAGING NEEDS

Ruler, pencil, craft knife, cutting mat, all-purpose glue, cellophane or clingfilm, scissors

Piece of medium-weight cardboard 25.5 by 43.5 cm (10 by 17 in)

Tartan wrapping paper

1.2 m (1⅓ yd) tartan ribbon, 6.5 cm (2½ in) wide

RECIPE: Scottish shortbread

Preheat the oven to 180°C (350°F/Gas 4). Lightly grease a 20 by 30 cm (8 by 12 in) tin with oil and lightly dust it with flour.

1 In a mixing bowl, rub the **butter** into the **flour** with your fingertips until it is well blended and the mixture resembles fine bread crumbs.

2 Stir in the **sugar** and **semolina,** then add the **vanilla essence.** Turn the mixture on to the work surface and knead for 3 minutes, or until the dough comes together and the cracks disappear.

3 Using the back of a large spoon, press the dough into the prepared tin and flatten the top. Prick the dough all over with a fork.

4 Using the back of a knife blade, mark the dough into nine rectangles. Draw a diagonal line across each one to make triangles. ▶

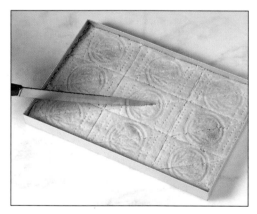

5 If you wish, press a wooden shortbread stamp on to the dough to imprint it with a thistle or other appropriate motif. It may help to put the stamp in the freezer for 30 minutes before you begin; this prevents the dough from sticking to the stamp.

6 Bake the dough in the preheated oven for 30 minutes or until it is golden in colour. Leave the shortbread to cool in the tin for about 15 minutes before cutting through the marked lines. Store the shortbread in an airtight container until you giftwrap it. ▪▪

GIFTWRAP: Tartan trimmings

Individually wrapped in cellophane or tartan paper, pieces of shortbread are packed in a recessed box tied with a colourful checked-ribbon bow.

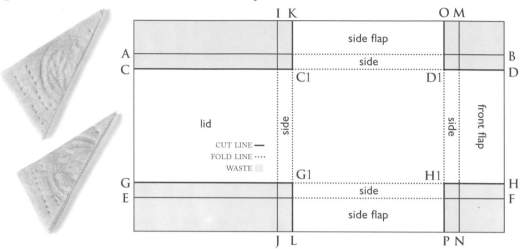

1 Using the template above as a guide, measure and draw two parallel lines 3.25 cm (1¼ in) and 5 cm (2 in), respectively, in from each of the long sides. These are marked A-B and C-D, and E-F and G-H on the template.

2 Measure and draw two parallel lines (I-J) 16 cm (6¼ in) and (K-L) 18 cm (7 in), respectively, in from one of the short sides. Measure and draw the last two parallel lines, (M-N) 5 cm (2 in) and (O-P) 7 cm (2¾ in) in from the opposite side.

3 With the cardboard placed flat on the cutting mat, score along all the marked lines, using the craft knife. These are where the cardboard is to be folded; take care not to cut through the lines at this stage.

4 Now cut along the inside lines at each corner. In this way you will remove two rectangles 5 by 7 cm (2 by 2¾ in), O-D1-D and P-H1-H, and two rectangles 5 by 18 cm (2 by 7 in), K-C1-C and L-G1-G.

5 Begin folding the box by bending up the outside lines to form the front and side flaps and the lid. Then fold along the inside lines to make the sides and base of the box.

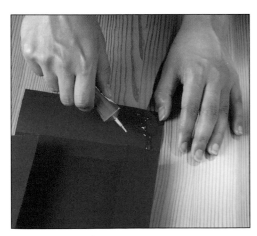

6 To create a recessed box, apply glue to the sides of the front flap and stick it to the side flaps.

7 Wrap each piece of shortbread in cellophane or clingfilm. (You do not need to do this if the tartan wrapping paper has a waxed finish.) Then wrap some of the shortbread in the tartan paper.

8 Arrange the shortbread in the box and close the lid. (You will have some pieces left over.) Tie the ribbon around the box, make a bow and trim the ends. ✻

CINNAMON AND NUT BARS

WITH A MOIST, NUTTY TEXTURE AND CRUNCHY STREUSEL TOPPING, these bars
are packed with cinnamon bundles and a slice of dried orange.

RECIPE INGREDIENTS

60g (2 oz) lightly salted butter

175g (6 oz) light brown sugar

1 large egg, lightly beaten

1 teaspoon grated orange rind

150g (5 oz) plain flour

1 teaspoon baking powder

1 teaspoon ground cinnamon

½ teaspoon salt

175g (6 oz) pecans

TOPPING

60g (2 oz) lightly salted butter

60g (2 oz) plain flour

60g (2 oz) light brown sugar

½ teaspoon ground cinnamon

1 teaspoon grated orange rind

Makes about 24 bars

PACKAGING NEEDS

Ruler, pencil, craft knife, cutting mat, scissors, tracing paper, masking tape, scrap of cardboard, pin, all-purpose glue, stapler

Piece of medium-weight cardboard 33 by 37.5 cm (13 by 15 in)

Double-sided tape, 5 cm (2 in) wide

Stencil of leaves and fruit (page 18)

Orange and green oil-based stencil sticks or stencil paints

Stencil brush

38 cm (15 in) stiff grosgrain ribbon, 2.5 cm (1 in) wide

6–8 small cinnamon sticks tied into two bundles with raffia

1 dried orange slice (page 26, step 6)

RECIPE: Cinnamon and nut bars

Preheat the oven to 190°C (375°F/Gas 5). Lightly grease a 20 cm (8 in) square baking tin with vegetable oil, such as sunflower oil.

1 In a medium-sized saucepan, melt the **butter.** Remove it from the heat and set it aside to cool slightly. Stir in the **sugar, egg** and **orange rind.**

2 Sift the **flour, baking powder, cinnamon** and **salt** into a mixing bowl, then pour in the sugar mixture.

3 On a chopping board, chop the **pecans** using a sharp knife. Add the nuts to the mixture in the bowl and stir to blend.

4 Turn the mixture into the prepared tin and level the top with a spatula. ▶

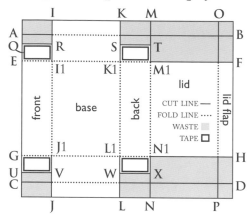

GIFTWRAP: Orange ribbons

Two stencilled ribbons of orange fruits and leaves decorate the box, which is made in one piece then packed with spicy nut bars and cinnamon sticks.

Template labels (box diagram):
I, K, M, O along top; A, B; Q, R, S, T; E, F; I1, K1, M1; **lid**; **front**, **base**, **back**, **lid flap**; CUT LINE —, FOLD LINE ····, WASTE ▨, TAPE ▢; G, H; U, V, W, X; J1, L1, N1; C, D; J, L, N, P

5 To make the topping, in a bowl rub the **butter** into the **flour** with your fingertips and stir in the **sugar, cinnamon** and **orange rind.** Sprinkle the topping over the mixture in the tin.

6 Bake in the preheated oven for 30 minutes, until the topping is set and browned. Using a sharp knife, cut into 24 bars while still warm. Leave to cool in the tin on a wire rack. ▪▪

1 Using the template above as a guide, measure and draw with a pencil lines A-B and C-D, 2.5 cm (1 in) in from each of the long sides of the cardboard, and two more, parallel lines, E-F and G-H, 5 cm (2 in) in from each of these. (This is the right side of the box, so make the lines faint.) Measure and draw a line, I-J, 5 cm (2 in) in from one of the short sides. Then draw a parallel line, K-L, 12.5 cm (5 in) in from that, M-N a further 5 cm (2 in) in, and O-P 12.5 cm (5 in) in. This last line will be 2.5 cm (1 in) from the edge of the cardboard.

2 There will be four 5 cm (2 in) squares on the cardboard. Draw a line 2 cm (¾ in) in from the outer line in each case, Q-R, S-T, U-V and W-X.

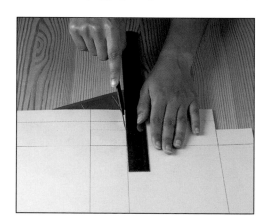

3 Use a craft knife to cut away the corner sections I-R-Q and J-V-U. Cut away the portions marked by points F-M1-T-S-K and H-N1-X-W-L, respectively. Cut through the following: R-I1, V-J1, S-K1 and W-L1.

4 Cut four 3 cm (1¼ in) pieces of double-sided tape, peel off the backing and stick them on the areas Q-R-I1-E, S-T-M1-K1, U-V-J1-G and W-X-N1-L1. Cut a liner out of tracing paper for the box. Follow lines E-G-J1-V-W-L1-N1-M1-K1-S-R-I1-E.

5 Trace the stencil on page 18 on tracing paper and cut out the outline, using a craft knife. The stencils form a ribbon pattern from the edge of the lid flap, across the top, back, base and front of the box. Position the stencil 3 cm (1¼ in) in from one outer edge, F-M1, and parallel to it. Secure it with masking tape.

6 Follow the instructions for the type of stencil colour you use. For oil-based sticks rub a little colour on to a scrap of cardboard, then rub the brush on to the colour. Stencil the leaf and fruit pattern, then mark through the stencil repeat holes with a pin. Reposition the stencil and complete the pattern.

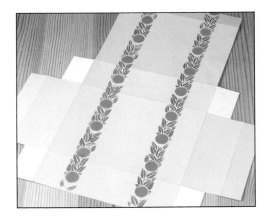

7 Position the stencil 3 cm (1¼ in) in from the opposite edge and colour the pattern in the same way. Set aside until the paint has dried. Using a craft knife, score along the pencil lines.

8 Fold the box along the scored lines. Starting with the inner sections, peel off the paper on the double-sided tape; press overlapping sections in place. Cut the sides of the front flap diagonally so the box closes easily (see page 16).

9 With the ribbon, make three loops, each smaller than the last; then staple the centre. Glue the bow to the top of the box. Place the liner in the box and stack the bars inside, along with the cinnamon bundles and dried orange slice. 🎁

GINGER AND HONEY FAIRINGS

GOLDEN BROWN AND GLISTENING WITH SPECKS OF EDIBLE GOLD LEAF, these
biscuits were traditionally sold at country fairs in Victorian England – hence their name.

RECIPE INGREDIENTS

125 g (4 oz) plain flour

1 teaspoon baking powder

1 teaspoon bicarbonate of soda

2 teaspoons ground ginger

¾ teaspoon ground cinnamon

¼ teaspoon grated nutmeg

Dash ground allspice

60 g (2 oz) cold lightly salted butter, diced

60 g (2 oz) caster sugar

2 tablespoons (30 ml) honey, plus extra for brushing

Edible gold leaf, to decorate

Makes about 15 biscuits

PACKAGING NEEDS

Wire cutters or pliers, scissors, all-purpose glue, pencil, craft knife, cutting mat, elastic band

25 cm (10 in) medium-gauge florist's wire

2 wire rings, 12.5 cm (5 in) in diameter

4 m (4¼ yards) gold metallic ribbon, 3 mm (⅛ inch) wide

Pair of compasses (optional)

Piece of gold-coloured cardboard, about 15 by 15 cm (6 by 6 in)

½ m (½ yd) gold sequin trim, 8.25 cm (3¼ in) wide

Piece of cellophane 30 by 30 cm (12 by 12 in)

Gold-coloured gauze or net 50 by 50 cm (20 by 20 in)

RECIPE: Ginger and honey fairings

Preheat the oven to 200°C (400°F/Gas 6). Lightly grease baking sheets with butter.

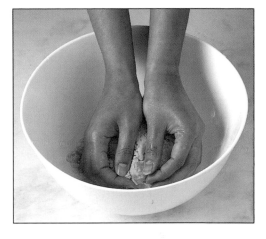

1 Sift the **flour, baking powder, soda** and **spices** into a mixing bowl. Add the **butter** and rub it in until the mixture resembles fine crumbs.

2 Stir in the **sugar** and **honey.** Then form the dough into a ball and knead it lightly, in the bowl, until it is smooth and free of cracks.

3 Pull off pieces of the dough and roll them on the work surface with your hand, shaping them into balls the size of a walnut.

4 Place the dough balls 7.5 cm (3 in) apart on the baking sheets – they will spread while baking. Flatten the balls slightly with a fork. ▶

5 Bake in the preheated oven for 6 to 7 minutes, until the biscuits are golden brown. Leave the biscuits to cool for 2 to 3 minutes, then transfer them to a wire rack using a spatula. While they are still warm, brush the tops of the biscuits with melted honey.

6 Tear small pieces of **gold leaf** and, using a small craft brush, press them on top of each biscuit. ▪▪

GIFTWRAP: All that glitters

A package worthy of the most glittering occasion is unwrapped to reveal a wire-frame container covered with sequin trim and full of sparkling biscuits.

1 Using wire cutters, cut the florist's wire into three pieces. To make the frame, twist one end of the pieces of wire around one wire ring. Twist the other ends around the other ring so that the rings are 8.25 cm (3¼ in) apart.

2 Cut 1 m (1 yd) off the metallic ribbon for the bow. Fix one end of the remaining ribbon on to one of the wire rings with a dab of glue. Bind the ribbon around to cover the ring; repeat for the other ring and the uprights, so the frame is totally covered.

3 With the compasses, or using the wire frame as a guide, draw a circle on the back of the cardboard. Using a craft knife, cut it out to fit the base of the frame exactly.

4 Apply some glue to the edge of the cardboard, gold side up, and glue the base of the frame to the board.

5 Working on a small section of the frame at a time, squeeze a little glue on to the outside of the top and bottom rings. Press the sequin trim on to the glued sections and, keeping the trim taut, stick it all around to cover the frame. Allowing for a slight overlap, trim the end of the strip and glue it in place.

6 Press the square of cellophane into the wire-frame container, arrange the biscuits inside and draw the corners of the paper over the top.

7 To wrap the container, place it in the centre of the gold net and bring the four corners over the top. Gather the net at the top of the frame and secure with an elastic band.

Note

For a ready-made frame, you can use a drum-shaped wire lampshade frame about 12.5 cm (5 in) in diameter. All you have to do is use wire cutters to cut the bulb holder from the frame and discard the pieces. Then cover the frame with gold metallic ribbon as described.

8 Cut the remaining metallic ribbon in half and place the two pieces together. Tie a bow around the elastic band. 🎁

LEMON SUGAR-CRYSTAL BUNS

WITH THEIR SHARP CITRUS TANG and glistening sugar-crystal topping, these buns are light and refreshing. The dried lemon slices packed with them in a wooden basket hint at their flavour.

RECIPE INGREDIENTS

90 g (3 oz) lightly salted butter,
at room temperature

125 g (4 oz) caster sugar

Grated rind of 1 lemon

125 g (4 oz) plain flour

125 g (4 oz) cornflour

1 teaspoon baking powder

2 large eggs, lightly beaten

1 teaspoon (5 ml) lemon juice

About 1 tablespoon (15 ml) milk (optional)

About 2 tablespoons large
coffee-sugar crystals

DECORATION

2 lemons, thinly sliced

Makes 12 buns

PACKAGING NEEDS

Rubber gloves, polishing cloth, colourless
wax furniture polish, scissors

Wooden basket with a handle; the one used
here is 15 by 20 cm (6 by 8 in)

Bright yellow and white emulsion paints or
acrylic water-based paints

2 small containers, such as foil tart tins, for
the paint

Medium-grade wire wool

Small piece of sponge

Thin wire

Fresh or dried bay leaves

Piece of green and white checked cotton,
30 by 40 cm (12 by 16 in)

RECIPE: Lemon sugar-crystal buns

Preheat the oven to 220°C (425°F/Gas 7). Lightly grease 12 small bun tins.

1 In a mixing bowl, beat the **butter** with a wooden spoon until it is light and creamy. Then beat in the **sugar** and **lemon rind** until blended.

2 In another bowl, sift together the **flour, cornflour** and **baking powder**. Add the dry ingredients and beaten **eggs** alternately to the butter and sugar, stirring well between additions.

3 Stir in the **lemon juice** and a little **milk,** if needed, so the batter drops easily from the spoon when the spoon is lifted from the bowl.

4 Spoon the batter into the prepared tins and sprinkle the **sugar crystals** on top of each one. ▶

5 Bake in the preheated oven for about 10 minutes, until the buns are firm and springy to the touch. Leave to cool slightly in the tins, then transfer them to a wire rack to cool completely. Store the buns in an airtight container until you are ready to pack them.

6 To dry the **lemon slices** for the decoration, spread them in a single layer on a wire rack. Place the rack in the oven at 130°C (250°F/ Gas ½) for 2 to 3 hours, until the slices are dry. Leave the slices on the rack in a warm dry place, such as an airing cupboard, overnight. ■

GIFTWRAP: Springtime colours

Painted bright daffodil yellow and decorated with dried lemon slices and scented leaves, this wooden basket will be a practical addition to the home.

1 Pour a little of the yellow paint into one of the containers. Put on the rubber gloves, break off a piece of wire wool about 5 cm (2 in) square and crumple it into a pad.

2 Dab the wire wool into the paint and, following the grain of the wood, rub in the paint with a few firm strokes. This will both smooth and colour the wood in one process.

3 Continue in this way until the basket and handle are painted inside and out. If you would like to leave more of the natural wood showing through, apply the paint thinly and use a clean pad of wire wool to remove some of it. Let the basket dry.

4 Pour a little of the white paint into the other container. Dampen the sponge with water, squeeze out any excess and dip it into the paint. Dab the sponge all over the basket, leaving some of the yellow colour showing through to give a mottled effect.

5 Leave the basket to dry thoroughly. Then, using the polishing cloth, apply the furniture polish and rub it all over the basket. If you would like a glossier finish, apply a second coat of polish.

6 To make the decoration, cut a piece of wire about 15 cm (6 in) long. Thread two or three dried lemon slices and bay leaves alternately on to the wire and arrange them into an attractive cluster.

7 Tie the lemon and bay leaf decoration on to one side of the basket handle and twist the free ends of the wire together neatly at the back.

8 To finish the edges of the piece of cotton, fold the raw edges over to one side. Then line the basket with the cotton, with the folded sides facing downwards.

9 Arrange the buns in the finished painted basket, together with the remaining lemon slices and a few bay leaves. 🎁

Note

As an alternative to the wooden basket, you could use a woven basket. Once the lemon sugar-crystal buns have been eaten, the basket, with its liner, can be used for serving bread or rolls.

CHEESE SHELLS

MEDITERRANEAN-STYLE SAVOURY SNACKS are perfect to serve with drinks. The scallop shells they are baked in and the shell-topped box continue the seaside theme.

RECIPE INGREDIENTS

150g (5oz) plain flour

Pinch salt

75g (2½oz) semolina

125g (4oz) cold unsalted butter

125g (4oz) Parmesan cheese, freshly and finely grated

60g (2oz) sun-dried tomatoes in oil

1 tablespoon chopped fresh basil

2–4 tablespoons (30–60ml) cold water

8 scallop shells or shell-shaped baking dishes or mini tart pans

Makes 8 shell-shaped cheese snacks

PACKAGING NEEDS

Saucer, cotton bud, pencil, tracing paper, masking tape, piece of cardboard, colourless wax furniture polish, polishing cloth, all-purpose glue, greaseproof paper

Round wooden box with swing handle and lid; the one used here is 18cm (7in) in diameter and 14cm (5½in) deep

Lilac-blue emulsion paint or acrylic water-based paint

Pink dry-brush paint or water-based paint

2 small pieces of sponge

Stencils of shell designs (page 31)

Stencil brush

6 or 7 decorative shells

Tissue paper, to line box

RECIPE: Cheese shells

Preheat the oven to 180°C (350°F/Gas 4). Lightly brush eight scrubbed and dried scallop shells with oil and dust them with flour, shaking off the excess.

1 Mix together the **flour, salt** and **semolina** in a mixing bowl and rub in the **butter** with your fingertips until the mixture is like fine crumbs. Stir in the **cheese** with a knife.

2 Pat the **tomatoes** dry with paper towel and chop them finely. Add them to the butter mixture.

3 Stir in the **basil** and enough **water** to make a dough. Knead the dough in the bowl until it is smooth, then divide it into eight equal portions.

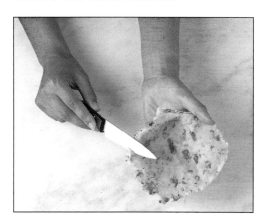

4 On a floured surface, roll out each portion of dough to about the size of a shell. Lightly press the dough into each of the prepared shells and trim the edges with a sharp knife. ▶

5 Stand the shells on baking sheets and bake them in the preheated oven for 20 minutes, or until they are golden brown.

6 Leave the snacks in their shells to cool for about 15 minutes. Loosen around the edges with a knife and carefully turn them out on to a wire rack; leave until completely cool. Store them between layers of greaseproof paper in an airtight tin. ▪

GIFTWRAP: A shell collection

The cheese shells are packed in a wooden box with a swing handle, reminiscent of a beach bucket. The stencilled shell decoration hints at what might be inside.

1 Remove the box lid and set it aside. Pour a little of the lilac-blue paint on to a saucer. Squeeze the sponge and lightly dampen it with water, squeezing out any excess. Then dip the sponge into the paint.

3 Use a cotton bud dipped in paint to reach the difficult areas around the handle. Leave the paint to dry.

2 Using stroking movements and working in the direction of the grain, apply the paint to the side and base of the box.

4 Turn the box upside-down and mark the centre front with a pencil to make it easier to position the stencil.

5 Trace and cut out the shell stencils. Position the scallop shell on the centre front of the box and anchor it with masking tape. Use a stencil brush to apply the pink dry-brush paint, following the directions on the product. If you are using water-based paint, apply it with a sponge as before, dabbing off any excess on the cardboard. Leave the paint to dry.

8 Glue a cluster of shells on to the centre of the lid.

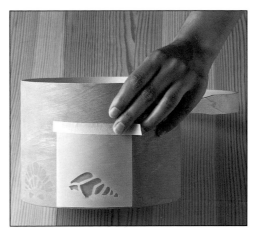

6 Work out where you want to place the other shell stencils around the box. Position the next one with masking tape and apply the paint as before. Allow the paint to dry before moving the stencil and painting the rest.

9 Line the box with crumpled tissue paper and carefully place the shells inside. If it is likely to be a while before the box is opened, put greaseproof paper between each one. ❖

7 Polish the lid and handle of the box and, when all the shell patterns are dry, polish the box, using two applications of polish if you prefer a glossier finish.

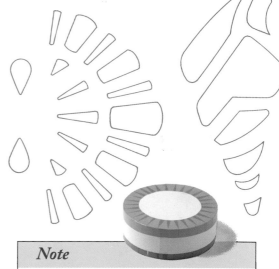

Note

If you cannot find a box with a handle, you could make a round box following the general instructions on pages 8–9, or use a ready-made papier-mâché one.

Viennese Alphabet Biscuits

Make these shaped biscuits to spell out a name or a seasonal greeting,
or make them all in the more traditional letter 'S' shape.

RECIPE INGREDIENTS

150 g (5 oz) lightly salted
butter, softened

75 g (2½ oz) icing sugar, plus
extra for dusting

Pinch salt

Grated rind of ½ orange

2 large egg yolks, lightly beaten,
plus one, lightly beaten, for glazing

215 g (7 oz) plain flour

Makes about 26 biscuits

PACKAGING NEEDS

Ruler, paper glue, hole punch, scissors, tape

Piece of medium-weight wrapping paper;
for the dimensions used here
25 by 35 cm (9¾ by 13¾ in)

Rectangular box to use as a model; the one
used here measures 15 x 10 x 4.75 cm
(6 x 4 x 1⅞ in)

50 cm (20 in) thick shiny cord, for handles

Edible gold powder (optional)

Small craft brush (optional)

Cellophane or a polythene bag

One alphabet biscuit, the initial of
the recipient

½ m (½ yd) gold metallic ribbon, 3 mm
(⅛ in) wide

RECIPE: Viennese alphabet biscuits
Oven temperature 190°C (375°F/Gas 5). Line baking sheets with greaseproof paper.

1 Put the **butter** into a mixing bowl. Sift in the **icing sugar** and **salt**, add the **orange rind** and two **egg yolks** and beat, using an electric beater or wooden spoon, until smooth.

2 Sift in the **flour** and mix to form a firm dough. Knead until the dough is smooth and free of cracks. Wrap the dough in aluminium foil and chill in the refrigerator for at least 4 hours, or overnight.

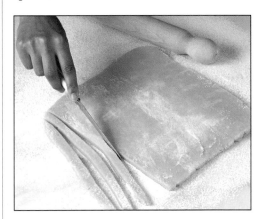

3 Preheat the oven and prepare the baking sheets. Unwrap the dough, sprinkle it and the work surface with sifted icing sugar and roll out the dough to a thickness of 1 cm (⅜ in). Cut the dough into strips 1 cm (⅜ in) wide.

4 Gather any trimmings together, roll them out again and cut more strips. Using your fingers, roll the strips lightly on the work surface to make them round. ▶

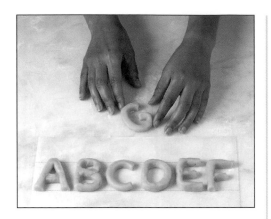

5 Draw two lines 5 cm (2 in) apart on baking parchment. Use the lines as a guide to shape the strips into letters; the dough is soft and larger shapes will break. Press the dough gently to smooth over any seams. Using a spatula, place the letter shapes well apart on the baking sheets and brush the tops with the extra egg yolk.

6 Bake in the preheated oven for 10 minutes, or until the biscuits are golden brown. Leave them to cool and firm up slightly, then transfer them to a wire rack to cool completely. ▪▪

GIFTWRAP: Bags of gold

A stylish carrier bag made of marbled paper with golden cord handles is personalised with a gold-brushed alphabet biscuit for decoration.

1 Fold one long edge of the paper 1.5 cm (½ in) to the wrong side. Glue in place.

3 Fold under the excess paper at the bottom of the box, as you would when wrapping a present, and glue the overlaps in place. Carefully remove the box from the bag.

2 Place the paper right side down on the work surface. Place the box on the paper so that its top edge is aligned with the folded edge of the paper. Wrap the paper around the box and glue the overlap.

4 Using the hole punch, make two holes on each side of the bag, close to the top and about 4 cm (1½ in) apart.

5 To make the handles, cut the cord in half and bind the four ends with tape to prevent them from fraying. From the inside, thread the two ends of one length of cord through the punched holes on one side of the bag.

6 Knot the ends on the outside of the bag, peel off the tape and trim the ends. Make the other handle in the same way.

7 If you wish, brush the biscuits with the edible gold powder, using a small craft brush.

8 To prevent the biscuits from staining the marbled bag, use the cellophane to make a smaller bag to put them in. Reserve one biscuit for the decoration. Seal the top of the cellophane bag with tape and place it in the carrier bag.

9 Tie the reserved biscuit to one of the handles on the carrier bag, using the metallic ribbon. 🎁

—35—

COCONUT WREATH BISCUITS

As decorative as they are delicious, these biscuits also make attractive Christmas tree ornaments. Emphasise the festive theme by tying some with narrow red or green ribbons.

RECIPE INGREDIENTS

125 g (4 oz) plain flour

60 g (2 oz) caster sugar

60 g (2 oz) desiccated coconut

*30 g (1 oz) lightly salted butter,
at room temperature*

1 large egg, lightly beaten

About 2 tablespoons (30 ml) milk

Red and green glacé cherries, to decorate

*2 biscuit cutters, 5 cm (2 in) and 2.5 cm (1 in)
in diameter*

Makes about 25 biscuits

PACKAGING NEEDS

*Scissors, all-purpose glue, iron, needle and
thread, small polythene bag*

*Wooden box, sold as a desk tidy; the
one used here is 9 x 9 x 12 cm
(3½ x 3½ x 4¾ in)*

Fine sandpaper

Red matt paint

Small paintbrush

*Piece of thick cardboard 7.5 by 9 cm
(3 by 3½ in)*

*Piece of cotton gingham 53 by 53 cm
(21 by 21 in)*

*Double-sided tape, 5 cm
(2 in) wide*

*45 cm (½ yd) thin cord in each of two
coordinated shades*

RECIPE: Coconut wreath biscuits

Preheat the oven to 190°C (375°F/Gas 5). Line baking sheets with baking parchment.

1 In a mixing bowl, combine the **flour, sugar, coconut, butter** and **egg** using a wooden spoon. Stir in just enough **milk** to make a firm dough.

2 On a lightly floured surface, roll out the dough to a thickness of 6 mm (¼ in). Cut out circles with a 5 cm (2 in) round biscuit cutter, pressing the cutter firmly straight down into the dough. Do not twist or turn the cutter, or the shape will be spoiled.

3 Using a 2.5 cm (1 in) round biscuit cutter, cut out the middles of the circles in the same way. Gather up the trimmings, roll them out again and cut out more rings. You will have about 25 rings.

4 Using a small sharp knife, cut the **cherries** into little crescent-shaped pieces. ▶

5 Place the dough rings on the prepared baking sheets and decorate with the pieces of cherry, alternating the red and green.

6 Bake the rings in the preheated oven for about 12 minutes, or until they begin to turn light brown at the edges. Let the biscuits cool for 5 minutes on the baking sheets, then transfer to a wire rack with a metal spatula. ▪▪

GIFTWRAP: In the bag

The colourful coconut rings are presented together with two lasting gifts, a painted wooden box and a cotton gingham bag.

1 Lightly sandpaper the surface of the wooden box to provide a base for the paint, then dust it. Paint the outside of the box with the red paint and let it dry. Apply a second coat if necessary, and let it dry.

3 With the fabric right side down, peel off the backing strips and press the cardboard quickly and firmly on to the centre of the panel. Fold over the sides of the fabric and stick them down on to the back of the cardboard.

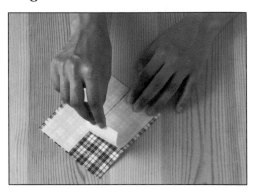

2 Cut a piece of gingham 10 by 12.5 cm (4 by 5 in) and cover the wrong side with double-sided tape. Position the cardboard in the centre and draw around it. Cut away quarter-circle shapes from the corners of the fabric up to the corners, to reduce bulk when the edges are turned in.

4 Stick the cloth panel on to the centre of one side of the box, and glue one of the biscuits to it, using the all-purpose glue.

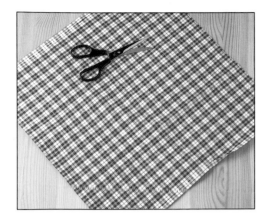

5 To make the bag, cut a piece of fabric 40 cm (16 in) square. Turn 6 mm (¼ in) to the wrong side along each side of the fabric and iron in place. For the top of the bag, take one side of the material and turn over 6 cm (2¼ in) to the wrong side. Sew a hem, either by hand or using a sewing machine.

6 With the right sides together, and the hem at the top, fold the bag in half so that the two side edges meet. Leaving a 6 mm (¼ in) seam, sew the edges together, to make the centre back of the bag.

7 To finish the bag, sew a 6 mm (¼ in) seam along the bottom. Turn the bag right side out.

8 Tie a knot in each end of both lengths of cord. Hold the two pieces of cord together and find the middle point. Sew the cords to the back of the bag, over the centre back seam and level with the top hem.

9 Place the polythene bag inside the cotton one and press it into the box. Fill the bag with biscuits and tie the cords around the top. 🎁

Note

You could present the biscuits in the checked bag alone, or make a cardboard box of dimensions similar to those of the wooden one and either paint it red or cover it with red giftwrap. For a seasonal gift, turn the biscuits into Christmas tree decorations by looping red or green ribbon through the central hole of each wreath.

SPICED GINGERBREAD PEOPLE

GINGERBREAD MEN AND WOMEN ARRANGED in a circle in a polka-dot box make a fun gift.
Include the cutters, and your box can be repopulated.

RECIPE INGREDIENTS

175 g (6 oz) plain flour

Pinch salt

½ teaspoon bicarbonate of soda

1 teaspoon ground ginger

½ teaspoon ground cinnamon

½ teaspoon ground allspice

90 g (3 oz) unsalted butter, softened

2 tablespoons soft dark brown sugar

4 tablespoons (60 ml) molasses

3 tablespoons (45 ml) milk

Two 10 cm (4 in) gingerbread biscuit cutters

ICING

60 g (2 oz) icing sugar, sifted

2-3 teaspoons (10-15 ml) lemon juice or water

Assorted food colourings

Makes at least 8 biscuits

PACKAGING NEEDS

3 saucers, scissors, all-purpose glue, compasses (optional), craft knife, cutting mat

Wooden cheese box, about 35 cm (14 in) in diameter, or make a round cardboard box, following the instructions on pages 8–9

White emulsion paint

2 cm (¾ in) paintbrush

2 'tester' pots of blue and green emulsion paint

Small piece of sponge

1 m (1 yd) gossamer ribbon, 6.5 cm (2½ in) wide

½ m (½ yd) double-faced satin ribbon, 8 mm (⅜ in) wide

Piece of stiff cardboard, about 38 by 38 cm (15 by 15 in)

75 cm (30 in) paper ribbon, 9 cm (3½ in) wide

Tissue paper, to line box

RECIPE: Spiced gingerbread people

Oven temperature 190°C (375°F/Gas 5). Lightly brush baking sheets with oil.

1 Sift the **flour, salt, bicarbonate of soda** and **spices** into a bowl. In a separate bowl, beat the **butter, sugar** and **molasses** until well blended. Add the dry ingredients and **milk** alternately to the butter mixture and stir to make a dough.

2 Wrap the dough in greaseproof paper and chill it in the refrigerator for at least 2 hours. It is slightly sticky, but will become firmer with chilling.

3 Preheat the oven. On a lightly floured surface, roll out the dough to a thickness of 6 mm (¼ in).

4 Using the gingerbread biscuit cutters, cut out four men and four women shapes for the gift. Reroll the trimmings and cut some more shapes if you wish. ►

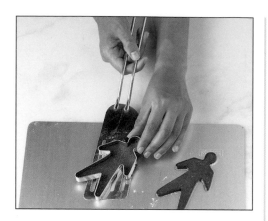

5 Arrange the shapes on the prepared baking sheets. Bake them in the preheated oven for 10 to 12 minutes, until they are beginning to darken at the edges. Let them cool slightly on the baking sheet, then transfer them to a wire rack.

6 To decorate the biscuits, mix the **icing sugar** to a stiff paste with the **lemon juice** or **water.** Colour it as you wish and spoon it into a piping bag fitted with a fine nozzle. Pipe features or the outlines of clothes or jewellery on to the gingerbread people. ▪▪

GIFTWRAP: Family circle

Pack the gingerbread family ring in a shallow wooden box painted with polka dots, and tie on one of the biscuit cutters as a fun extra.

1 Paint the outside of the box and lid with white emulsion paint, and set them aside to dry.

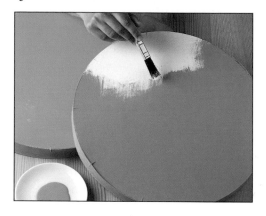

2 Put a little of each of the coloured paints into a small saucer or container. Then paint the box green and the lid blue, and leave them to dry.

3 Using a pair of scissors, cut out a circle about 5 cm (2 in) in diameter from the piece of sponge. This is the stamp for the white polka dots on the lid. Save the rest of the sponge for the next step.

4 Dip a small piece of sponge in the blue paint and dab it on to the box to create a slightly marbled effect. Let the paint dry. If you wish, you can marble the lid with green paint if you want to omit the white dots.

—42—

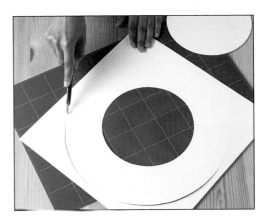

5 Pour a little white emulsion paint into a saucer. Lightly dip the sponge circle into the paint and stamp circles randomly all over the lid. Set the lid aside to dry.

6 Tie the wide gossamer ribbon in a bow and glue it to the lid. Trim the ends into 'V' shapes. Thread the narrow ribbon through one of the gingerbread cutters and tie the cutter to the bow.

7 Using the compasses, or two plates as a guide, draw a cardboard circle with an outer diameter of 30 cm (12 in) and an inner diameter of 23 cm (9 in) to fit in the box. Cut around the edges of the circles with a craft knife on a cutting mat.

8 Unravel the paper ribbon to its full width, then wrap it around the cardboard to cover the circle entirely. Use a piece of tape or glue to secure the ends.

9 In a small dish, mix a teaspoon of icing sugar into a paste with a couple of drops of water. Use this to stick the gingerbread men and women alternately around the ring. Line the box with crumpled tissue paper, and place the ring inside. 🎁

Note

For a more 'fairytale' presentation for a child, buy a stamp – for example, one of a teddy bear – and use it to decorate the lid in place of the white polka dots.

VANILLA AND PEPPERMINT BISCUITS

THE CONTRASTING COLOURS OF THE GREEN AND CREAM CHEQUERED BISCUITS are echoed
in the woven ribbon pattern that decorates the top of the two-tone cardboard box.

RECIPE INGREDIENTS

400 g (14 oz) plain flour

250 g (8 oz) sugar

½ teaspoon salt

125 g (4 oz) lightly salted butter, softened

2 large eggs, plus one for binding

2 teaspoons (10 ml) vanilla essence

3 drops edible yellow food colouring, or as desired

1 tablespoon (15 ml) peppermint cordial

8–10 drops edible green food colouring, or as desired

Makes about 24 biscuits

PACKAGING NEEDS

Ruler, pencil, craft knife, cutting mat, scissors, staple gun or stapler, tape, all-purpose glue

Piece of stiff cream cardboard 25 by 25 cm (10 by 10 in), for the box

Piece of stiff green cardboard 40 by 40 cm (16 by 16 in), for the lid

2 rolls double-sided tape, 1 cm (⅜ in) wide and 5 cm (2 in) wide

1.25 m (1¼ yd) each cream and green stiff grosgrain ribbon, 2.25 cm (⅞ in) wide

Tracing or greaseproof paper, for lining

RECIPE: Vanilla and peppermint biscuits

Oven temperature 200°C (400°F/Gas 6). Line baking sheets with greaseproof paper.

1 In a mixing bowl, beat together the **flour, sugar, salt, butter** and two **eggs** with a wooden spoon. Divide the dough in half and put one half into another bowl.

2 Add the **vanilla** and **yellow food colouring** to half the dough and knead until the colour is well blended. Form into a ball. Repeat with the **peppermint cordial** and **green colouring**. Wrap the balls separately in clingfilm and chill for at least 1 hour.

3 Roll out each piece of dough between greaseproof paper until 1 cm (⅜ in) thick. Using a clean ruler as a guide, cut the dough into strips 1 cm (⅜ in) wide. You need 12 strips of one colour, 13 of the other.

4 Place five dough strips on the work surface, alternating the colours. Brush the surface with beaten egg. Place another layer of strips on top, with green over yellow and so on. ▶

5 Continue alternating layers to build up a five-layer chequerboard. Pat the dough block firmly with your hands, then form any remaining dough into blocks. Place the blocks in the freezer for about 30 minutes. Preheat the oven. Using a sharp knife, cut the blocks into slices 1.5 cm (½ in) thick.

6 Place the dough slices on the baking sheets and bake in the preheated oven for 10 to 12 minutes, until the biscuits are light brown at the edges. Leave the biscuits to cool slightly, then transfer them to a wire rack. ▪

GIFTWRAP: Chequered ribbons

The woven ribbon panel gives a plain, uncovered gift box an elegant look. And when the biscuits are finished, it will make a pretty container for other things.

1 To make the base of the box, draw a 24 cm (9½ in) square on the cream cardboard. Measure and draw lines 4.5 cm (1¾ in) in from each of the four sides. Then, using a craft knife on a cutting mat, cut around the outer lines.

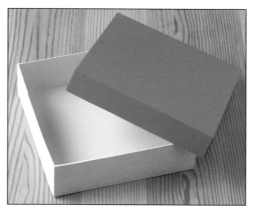

3 Make the box and lid, following the general instructions on pages 6–7.

2 For the box lid, draw a 20.5 cm (8⅛ in) square on the green card. Measure and draw lines 2.5 cm (1 in) in from each of the four sides. Cut around the outer lines as before.

4 To make the decorative panel, cut a 15.5 cm (6⅛ in) square of green cardboard. Measure and draw lines 2.5 cm (1 in) in from each side. Cut out the centre part, leaving a frame.

5 Cut two strips of the narrow double-sided tape to fit the edge of the frame. Stick the strips on to the back of the frame close to the outer edges on two opposite sides. Mark the centre of the frame with a pencil.

6 Cut five 14 cm (5½ in) strips of the ribbon in one colour (cream in the photographs). Peel off the covering from the tape. Starting at the centre, place the ribbon strips close together and parallel across the back of the frame. Press the ribbon edges on to the tape.

7 Cut five 14 cm (5½ in) strips of green ribbon and weave each one alternately under and over the cream ones. It may help to secure each ribbon individually with tape on the back of the frame.

8 Stick four strips of wide double-sided tape around the back of the frame to cover the ribbon ends. Peel off the covering, and stick the panel on to the box lid.

9 Place the two remaining strips of ribbon one on top of the other and make a loop about 7.5 cm (3 in) long. Holding it in the centre, make two more loops, each one smaller than the last, to form a six-loop bow.

10 Staple through the centre of the bow and trim the ribbon ends. Glue the bow at an angle across one corner of the box lid. Line the box with tracing paper, fill it with the biscuits and cover them with a square of tracing paper. ✤

Sweets & Candies

🎁 ANY OF THESE SWEET TREATS will make a welcome gift, perhaps as a birthday token or a personal thank you. They range from the instant pleasure of melt-in-the-mouth cranberry fudge and chocolate truffles to the longer-lasting chewiness of candied pecans, Turkish delight and pistachio nougat. Test your artistic skills by making small sugar-paste leaves or modelling miniature marzipan fruits. For no-cook delicacies try sugar-frosted fruits or chocolate coconut candies.

The gift-packing ideas, which will add immeasurably to the elements of surprise and delight, include the step-by-step transformation of household items such as wire baskets, metal cans, flowerpots and preserving jars into stylish and decorative containers. In addition, there are instructions for making a large-scale 'matchbox' and a simple coloured paper cone and for burnishing a ready-made wooden box to give an antique look.

CRANBERRY FUDGE

A PERFECT WINTER HOLIDAY GIFT, this fudge combines a delightful
sweetness with the sharp taste of the bright seasonal berries.

RECIPE INGREDIENTS

90 g (3 oz) cranberries

875 g (1¾ lb) granulated cane sugar

150 ml (¼ pint) milk

60 g (2 oz) lightly salted butter

1 teaspoon (5 ml) maple syrup

215 g (7½ oz) can full-cream sweetened condensed milk

1 teaspoon (5 ml) vanilla essence

Makes about 875 g (1¾ lb)

PACKAGING NEEDS

Tracing paper, tape, pencil, craft knife, cutting mat, masking tape, pressing cloth, iron, pins, hole punch, pen

Small rectangular wire container; the one used here measures 9 by 14 cm (3½ by 5½ in)

Tulip stencil and heart design (page 52)

White or cream cotton table napkin, about 30 by 30 cm (12 by 12 in)

Red and green fabric paints

Small dish, to use as palette

Stencil brush

Small piece of white cardboard 6 by 6 cm (2½ by 2½ in)

½ m (½ yd) cranberry-coloured double-faced satin ribbon, 3 mm (⅛ in) wide

RECIPE: Cranberry fudge
Lightly grease an 18 cm (7 in) square baking tin with vegetable oil.

1 Steam the **cranberries** over a saucepan of boiling water set over medium heat for 2 to 3 minutes, or until they are bright red. Remove them from the heat and allow to cool.

2 Put the **sugar, milk, butter** and **syrup** into a large, heavy-bottomed saucepan and stir over low heat until the sugar has dissolved. Increase the heat and bring to the boil, stirring all the time. Add the **condensed milk.**

3 Boil the mixture, still stirring, until it registers 116°C (240°F) on a sugar thermometer. Alternatively, drop some of the mixture into a cup of ice-cold water; it should form a soft ball that is easily flattened when pressed.

4 Remove the saucepan from the heat and stir in the cranberries and the **vanilla essence.** Continue stirring with a wooden spoon until the mixture begins to thicken. ▶

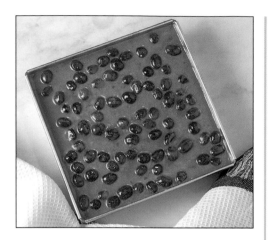

5 Pour the fudge into the prepared tin and let it cool and set for about 15 minutes.

6 Using a small sharp knife, mark the fudge into 2.5 cm (1 in) squares. Set the fudge aside to cool completely, then cut it and store the pieces in an airtight container until you are ready to giftwrap them. ▪▪

GIFTWRAP: In holiday mood

The simple wire container with its heart-shaped decoration will have a number of practical uses long after the confectionery has been eaten.

1 Place the tracing paper on the work surface and arrange the squares of fudge on it in a double layer to fit into the container (you will have some fudge left over). Wrap the parcel, securing the edges with tape.

2 On tracing paper, draw around the stencils below and cut them out with a craft knife on a cutting mat. Place the small tulip at one corner of the napkin and secure it with masking tape.

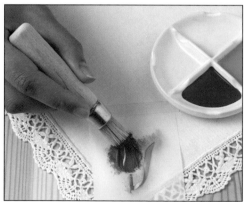

3 Pour a little paint into the dish. Working with a nearly dry brush, stencil the design in each corner. Let each colour dry for a few minutes before applying the next.

4 Securing the stencil as before, stencil the larger motif close to the centre of each edge of the napkin. Protecting the fabric with a pressing cloth, iron over the design with a cool iron to fix the paint.

5 Place the napkin right side up and fold the two sides to the centre. Press along the creases. Place the napkin folded side down and lay the parcel of fudge on top.

6 Wrap the parcel so that one edge of the napkin rests on the edge of the fudge parcel. Fold in the two ends and secure with pins.

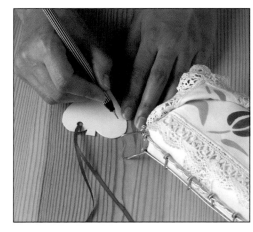

7 Place the napkin parcel in the container and open out the two corners on top to reveal one of the decorations along the napkin edge.

8 Using the stencil you have made, cut out a heart shaped gift tag from the white cardboard. Punch a hole in the tag and thread the ribbon through it. Write a message on one side and stencil a tulip bud and leaf on the other, then tie the tag to the container. 🎁

Note

You can also pack the fudge in other kitchen containers such as small baking tins, or you could make a rectangular box following the general instructions for making a square box on pages 6–7.

CHOCOLATE COCONUT CANDY

THESE CHOCOLATY REFRIGERATOR CANDIES look as if they have been lightly dusted with fine snow.
They are simple enough for young children to make with supervision.

RECIPE INGREDIENTS

125 g (4 oz) unsalted butter

*215 g (7 oz) plain chocolate,
broken into pieces*

60 g (2 oz) desiccated coconut

75 g (2½ oz) rolled oats

Icing sugar, sifted, for dusting

Small confectionery cases

Makes about 24 candies

PACKAGING NEEDS

*String, scissors, ruler, pencil, craft knife,
cutting mat, all-purpose glue*

*500 g (1 lb) food canister, washed and
thoroughly dried*

*Piece of corrugated cardboard, to wrap
around canister (see step 1)*

Double-sided tape, 5 cm (2 in) wide

*Piece of medium-weight cardboard, about
30 by 30 cm (12 by 12 in), for base and lid*

Ball of coarse string or paper cord

4 seed heads such as poppy, for decoration

Gold craft powder (optional)

Small craft brush (optional)

Tracing paper (optional)

RECIPE: Chocolate coconut candy
Line baking sheets with waxed paper.

1 Melt the **butter** and **chocolate** in a heatproof bowl set over a saucepan of boiling water. (It is not necessary to keep the saucepan over direct heat.)

2 As it melts, stir the butter and chocolate mixture with a wooden spoon, beating it until it is well blended and glossy.

3 Remove the bowl from the saucepan and dry the base with a tea towel. Stir in the **coconut** and **oats**, then set aside until the mixture cools.

4 Drop heaped teaspoonfuls of the mixture on to the lined baking sheets, using another teaspoon to ease the mixture off the spoon and shape it into walnut-sized balls. Put the sheets of candies into the refrigerator to harden for about 1 hour. ▶

5 Remove the candies from the refrigerator and sift the **icing sugar** over them to give a light dusting.

6 Carefully place the candies in individual confectionery cases, taking care not to shake off too much icing sugar as you do so. ▪

GIFTWRAP: All strung up

A metal food container wrapped in corrugated cardboard and finished with a string-covered lid and base has an informal, modern look that is just right.

1 Using a piece of string, measure the circumference of the container. Then use a ruler to measure the height. Cut a piece of corrugated cardboard to fit the container exactly. The container here was covered with a piece of cardboard 14.5 by 30 cm (5¾ by 12 in).

2 Cut a piece of double-sided tape exactly the length of the container (in this case 14.5 cm/5¾ in) and stick it on to the container.

3 Peel the backing strip off the tape and press one edge of the corrugated cardboard halfway across the strip. Wrap the cardboard tightly around the container and press the second edge on to the tape to meet the first one. Carefully measure the diameter of the container now that it is wrapped in cardboard. The one here measures 10 cm (4 in) wide.

4 To make the base and lid, cut two cardboard circles with the exact diameter of the covered tin, using a craft knife on a cutting mat. Then cut two side strips 2.5 cm (1 in) wide and 30 cm (12 in) long. Following the instructions on pages 8–9 for making a round box, make the box-like base and the lid in the same way.

5 To cover the cardboard base and lid (which are identical) with string or cord, spread the glue over the centre. Start in the middle with a tight coil of string and press it on to the glue. Applying more glue as you work, coil and press the string until the top and sides are covered. Cut off and glue the string end in place.

6 Spread glue over the inside of the string-covered base and press the container firmly into it.

7 Glue the seed heads on to the lid, and brush them with gold craft powder if you wish.

8 Fill the canister with the candies, and put on the lid. If you wish, you can cut circles of tracing paper to place between the layers of candies. 🎁

Note

To strike a brighter note, try using corrugated cardboard in primary colours. You could also experiment by making the corrugations run horizontally instead of vertically.

A Harvest of Marzipan Fruits

REALISTIC APPLES, PEARS, ORANGES AND BANANAS painted with food colouring and studded with clove stems are presented in a twig-topped box.

RECIPE INGREDIENTS

500 g (1 lb) granulated sugar

150 ml (¼ pint) water

Pinch cream of tartar

375 g (12 oz) ground almonds

2 large egg whites

90 g (3 oz) icing sugar, plus extra for attaching fruit (see page 61, step 7)

Red, green, orange, yellow and brown edible food colourings, paste or powder

Few drops of almond essence

Whole cloves for stems

Makes about 750 g (1½ lb) fruits

PACKAGING NEEDS

Rubber or cotton household gloves, colourless wax furniture polish, polishing cloth, all-purpose glue, ruler, pencil, scissors

Wooden box with a lid; the one used here is 15 x 11.5 x 5 cm (6 x 4½ x 2 in)

Orange emulsion paint or acrylic water-based paint

Gold paint

Medium-brown wood stain

3 small containers, such as foil tart tins

Medium-grade wire wool

Small, bare, forked twig

Tracing or greaseproof paper, to line box

Small confectionery cases

RECIPE: A harvest of marzipan fruits

Lightly brush a baking sheet with a lightly flavoured oil, such as sunflower oil.

1 Put the **sugar** and **water** into a large, heavy-based saucepan and stir continuously over low heat until the sugar has dissolved. Bring the syrup to the boil without stirring.

2 Dissolve the **cream of tartar** in a tablespoon of cold water, stir it into the syrup, and boil until it reaches 116°C (240°F) or the soft-ball stage (see page 75, step 3). Remove the pan from the heat and beat the syrup with a wooden spoon until it turns opaque.

3 Stir in the **ground almonds** and **egg whites.** Return the saucepan to low heat and stir for 2 to 3 minutes.

4 Pour the mixture on to the baking sheet, sift over the **icing sugar** and stir it in with a spatula. Allow the paste to cool, then knead it, sifting on a little more icing sugar if necessary, until it is pliable. ▶

5 Divide the paste into quarters. Add a dab of paste or pinch of powder **food colouring** to each one. Knead until uniformly coloured, adding more colour as desired. Sift icing sugar on to the work surface, and mould small pieces of the paste to represent the different fruits.

6 Dilute the food colouring in **almond essence** and brush it over the bananas, apples and pears to add shading. Lightly press the oranges over a fine grater to add texture. Press cloves into the fruit to make stems and bottoms. Leave the fruit to dry, then store them in an airtight container. ▪

GIFTWRAP: Golden glow

A wooden box painted in orange and brown and streaked with gold is decorated with a miniature 'tree' of marzipan fruits.

1 Pour a little of the orange and gold paints and the brown wood stain into separate containers.

2 Put on the rubber gloves. Tear off three pieces of wire wool, each about 5 cm (2 in) square, and shape them into pads.

3 Dab one of the wire wool pads into the orange paint and, following the grain of the wood, work in the paint with long, firm strokes to cover the sides and base of the box.

4 Without waiting for the paint to dry, rub gold paint over the orange. Then, again without allowing the paint to dry, rub in the wood stain and then another layer of gold paint.

5 Leave this final coat to dry, then rub over the box lightly with a small pad of clean wire wool. Repeat the same paint sequence on the lid and leave it to dry.

6 Polish the box and the lid with one or two coats of furniture polish, depending on how glossy you want the finish to be.

7 Glue the forked twig to the lid and allow to dry. Press on some of the marzipan fruits. Make a thick paste with a little icing sugar and water and use this to 'glue' the fruits on.

8 Cut two pieces of tracing paper to fit the base of the box. Cut a strip to go around the sides, 6 mm (¼ in) wider than the depth. Fold in the excess, snip into it so that the strip curves to fit inside the box. Fit one of the base shapes inside to cover the snipped paper.

9 Arrange a layer of confectionery cases in the box, put in an assortment of fruit and cover them with the second paper shape. Arrange another layer of paper cases and fruit on top. 🎁

Note

You can vary the choice of fruit decoration according to your mood or the recipient's taste. Try making an apple orchard or a colourful fruit salad.

CHOCOLATE RUM TRUFFLES

ROLLED IN COCOA POWDER OR CHOCOLATE VERMICELLI, these rich,
creamy truffles are every chocoholic's dream.

RECIPE INGREDIENTS

150 ml (¼ pint) double cream

275 g (9 oz) plain chocolate, broken into squares

2–3 tablespoons (30–45 ml) dark rum

3–4 tablespoons chocolate vermicelli

3–4 tablespoons cocoa powder

Makes about 24 truffles

PACKAGING NEEDS

Ruler, pencil, scissors, elastic band, craft knife, cutting mat, hole punch

Piece of medium-weight cardboard, at least 12.5 by 20 cm (5 by 8 in), for template and gift tag

Silver and coloured foil

Silver-coloured wire kitchen basket 15 cm (6 in) in diameter

Silver net or gauze 45 by 45 cm (18 by 18 in)

1.5 m (1½ yd) silver metallic ribbon, 3 mm (⅛ in) wide

60 cm (24 in) silver metallic ribbon, 8 mm (⅜ in) wide

Tissue paper, to match the coloured foil, to cover gift tag

Double-sided tape, 5 cm (2 in) wide

Silver marker pen

RECIPE: Chocolate rum truffles

1 Pour the **cream** into a heavy-bottomed saucepan and, over low heat, bring it just to the boil.

2 Remove the saucepan from the heat and, using a wooden spoon, stir in the **chocolate**. Return to the heat and stir until the chocolate melts.

3 Remove the saucepan from the heat and stir in the **rum**. Pour the mixture into a small, deep bowl and then cover. Set aside to cool for about 1 hour, then chill the mixture for at least 1 hour, or until the chocolate has set.

4 Using a melon baller 2 cm (¾ in) in diameter, scoop out balls of the mixture and place them on a piece of greaseproof paper. Between scoops, dip the baller in warm water so that the truffles come off more easily. You can also use the tip of a knife to ease them off. ▶

5 Spread the **chocolate vermicelli** on a piece of greaseproof paper. Roll half of the truffles one at a time in the vermicelli, lifting the corner of the paper to coat each truffle thoroughly.

6 Sift half the **cocoa powder** on to another piece of greaseproof paper. Place one uncoated truffle at a time on the paper and sift some of the remaining powder over it to cover. Store the truffles in airtight containers in the refrigerator until you are ready to giftwrap them. ❖

GIFTWRAP: A goody basket

A silver-coloured basket from the kitchenware department and glittering foil wrappers make this a gift that will shine in any company.

1 Make a 10 cm (4 in) square template on the piece of cardboard, saving the remaining card for the gift tag. Draw around the template on the two foils. Using scissors, cut out 12 squares in each colour of foil.

2 Wrap each truffle in a square of foil, folding over the edges neatly and pressing the wrapper close over the truffle. If you like, you can colour-code the foil according to which type of truffle you are wrapping.

3 Pile the truffles into the basket, alternating the different-coloured wrappers to best effect.

4 Place the basket in the centre of the net and gather the net around the neck of the basket, beneath the handle. Use an elastic band to secure it.

5 Cut off 60 cm (24 in) of the narrow ribbon and put it together with the wider one. Use the ribbons to tie the net under the basket handle.

6 To make the gift tag, cut a rectangle 5 by 7.5 cm (2 by 3 in) from the cardboard. Cut off two corners at an angle on one short side.

7 Cut a piece of the tissue paper 6 mm (¼ in) larger all round than the cardboard. Place the card in the centre of the tissue paper and fold over the edges of the paper, turning in the corners to give a neat edge.

8 Cut a piece of double-sided tape to cover the card and stick it on to the wrong side. Cut a piece of tissue paper exactly the same size as the tape. Peel off the backing strip and press the tissue paper on to it.

9 Using a hole punch, make a single hole in the shaped end of the gift tag. Write a message with the silver marker pen.

Note

Instead of using the wire container, you could package the truffles in a square of cellophane.

10 Thread the remaining ribbon through the hole in the gift tag and loop it around the handle of the basket. Tie a neat bow to attach the tag to the parcel. ⚘

ROSE-PETAL AND ORANGE TURKISH DELIGHT

KNOWN AS *LOUKOUMI* IN GREECE AND *RAHAT LOKUM*, meaning 'giving rest to the throat', in Turkey,
this sweet, presented in a box that hints at the contents, certainly lives up to its English name.

RECIPE INGREDIENTS

300 ml (½ pint) water

33 g (1¼ oz) powdered gelatin

375 g (12 oz) granulated sugar

*30 g (1 oz) candied orange peel,
finely chopped*

2 teaspoons (10 ml) orange juice

Orange edible food colouring

*1 tablespoon shelled pistachios,
roughly chopped*

2 teaspoons (10 ml) rosewater

Pink edible food colouring

Icing sugar, for dusting

PACKAGING NEEDS

*Ruler, felt-tip pen, pencil, craft knife,
cutting mat, all-purpose glue, scissors,
tracing or greaseproof paper, tape*

*Metal box or cardboard box covered with
aluminium foil; the metal box used here is
12.5 x 12.5 x 5 cm (5 x 5 x 2 in)*

*Piece of thin pink cardboard, about
10 by 20 cm (4 by 8 in)*

*Piece of thin beige cardboard, about
10 by 20 cm (4 by 8 in)*

*1 m (1 yd) each pale and dark pink
sheer ribbon, 5 cm (2 in) wide*

RECIPE: Rose-petal and orange Turkish delight

*Use two pieces of thick foil to line and divide an 18 cm (7 in) baking tin.
Fold up the central edges to create a strong partition to separate the flavours.*

1 Pour the **water** into a saucepan, sprinkle on the **gelatin** and dissolve over a low heat, stirring constantly with a wooden spoon. Add the **sugar** and stir until it dissolves.

2 Increase the heat and bring the mixture to the boil, then boil rapidly for 10 minutes, until the syrup is clear. Remove the saucepan from the heat and pour half the syrup into one jug, the other half into another jug.

3 Into one jug stir the chopped **orange peel** and **orange juice**. Add 1 or 2 drops of **orange food colouring** and stir until well blended.

4 Stir the chopped **pistachio nuts** and **rosewater** into the second jug of syrup and add 1 or 2 drops of **pink food colouring**. Stir until the mixture is well blended. ►•

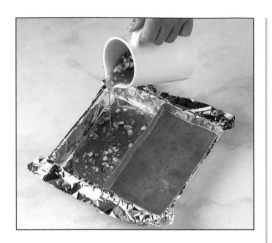

5 Pour the orange mixture into one half of the prepared tin and the pink mixture into the other half. Leave to set in a cool place, but not the refrigerator, for 24 hours.

6 Just before you pack the Turkish delight, sift some **icing sugar** on to the work surface. Turn the delight out of the tin and cut it into 2.5 cm (1 in) squares. Keeping the colours separate, sprinkle over more icing sugar to cover the pieces completely. ▪

GIFTWRAP: Squaring up

Echo the vibrant orange and pink colouring of the Turkish delight with an alternating pattern of squares glued to a metal or cardboard box.

1 If you are making a box, follow the instructions on pages 6–7. To cover this box with silver foil, follow the instructions on pages 114–15, steps 2–7, adjusting the measurements accordingly.

2 Using a ruler and felt-tip pen, measure and mark the top and sides of the lid into squares. Make sure the squares are equal in size and leave a small gap between them. Here, the squares are 2 cm (¾ in) long, with a 3 mm (⅛ in) gap.

3 On each piece of cardboard use a pencil and ruler to draw squares the same size as those on the lid. Use a craft knife on a cutting mat to cut out the squares. You will need 24 of one colour (here, pink), 21 of the other.

4 Glue alternate colours of cardboard on to the top of the lid, using the pen lines as a guide. Start at one corner, with a beige square, and work your way around the outside first.

5 When the top is completely covered, glue squares to the side of the lid. Remember to continue alternating the colours down the side – this is why you need more pink squares than beige ones.

6 Cut a piece of tracing paper to line the base of the box, and another to place between the layers. Pack the Turkish delight in two layers, with the colours alternating. Place the lid on the box.

7 To tie the ribbons across two opposite corners of the box, place the ribbons one on top of the other. Find the halfway mark on the ribbons and place this under one corner. Attach the ribbons to the base of the box with a strip of tape. Wind one end of the ribbons up over the next corner.

8 Continue winding the ribbons around the box. Take them under the next corner, securing with tape as before, then up on top of the box at the fourth corner. Tie a bow in the corner.

9 Adjust the bow and neatly trim the ends of the ribbons into a 'V' shape with scissors. ✤

FRENCH PISTACHIO NOUGAT

TRADITIONAL IN THE MONTELIMAR REGION OF FRANCE, this delicious sweet hides crunchy nuts in its colourful interior. Each piece is individually wrapped to keep it moist.

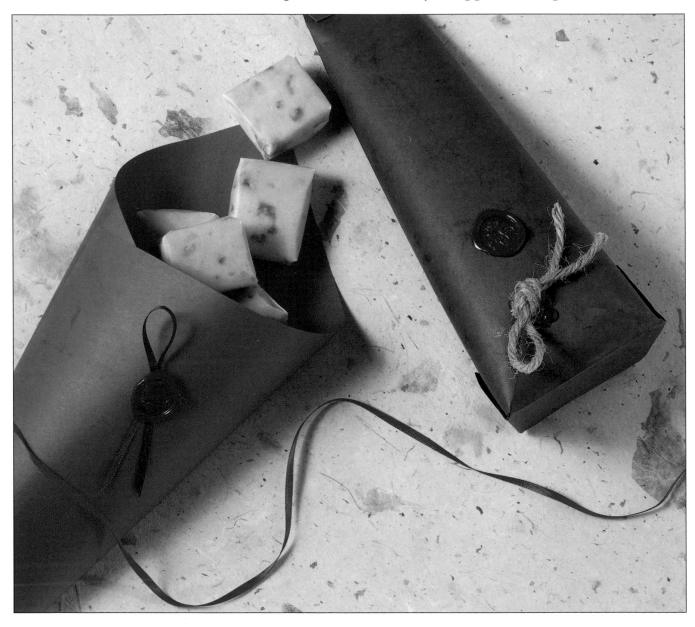

RECIPE INGREDIENTS

90g (3 oz) white set honey

3 large egg whites, beaten until stiff

375g (12 oz) granulated sugar

150 ml (¼ pint) water

60g (2 oz) glucose

About 2 teaspoons (10 ml) rosewater

150g (5 oz) shelled pistachios, roughly chopped

90g (3 oz) glacé cherries, roughly chopped

Sugar thermometer

Piece of cardboard 20 by 20 cm (8 by 8 in), to put under weights (see page 72, step 5)

Tracing paper or cellophane, for wrapping

Makes about 750g (1½ lb) nougat

PACKAGING NEEDS

Stapler, old knife, safety matches

Piece of waxed or other stiff paper 25 by 25 cm (10 by 10 in)

Double-sided tape, 8 mm (³⁄₈ in) wide

25 cm (10 in) soft string or double-faced satin ribbon, 3 mm (⅛ in) wide

Sealing wax

Sealing wax scoop or an old teaspoon

Sealing wax stamp or small coin

RECIPE: French pistachio nougat

Line an 18 cm (7 in) square baking tin with greaseproof paper.

1 In a large heatproof bowl, melt the **honey** over a saucepan of simmering water. Add the **egg whites** and beat until the mixture thickens.

2 Put the **sugar, water** and **glucose** into a saucepan. Bring to the boil and heat to 130°C (266°F) on a sugar thermometer. Stir in the **rosewater.**

3 Pour the syrup into the honey mixture. Beat it, still over the saucepan of water, with a whisk for 30 to 40 minutes until it is thick, or until a little paste dropped into a cup of ice-cold water forms a hard ball.

4 Remove the saucepan from the heat and place the bowl on the work surface. Stir in the chopped **nuts** and **cherries.** ▶

5 Pour the mixture into the lined tin and level the top with the back of a large spoon. Dip the spoon in hot water to stop the mixture from sticking to the spoon. Cover the surface with waxed paper, then the cardboard, and put weights or heavy cans on top to press it evenly. Leave the nougat to set firmly.

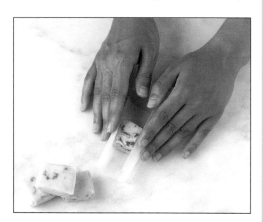

6 Mark the nougat into 2.5 cm (1 in) squares and cut it. Immediately wrap each square in tracing paper or cellophane to prevent it from drying out. ■

GIFTWRAP: Classic cones

Elegant blue paper cones can be made in minutes to elevate simple sweets into a delightful gift for any occasion.

1 Stick a piece of double-sided tape along one edge of the paper. Place the paper so that the taped edge is on your right, ready to make the cone shape.

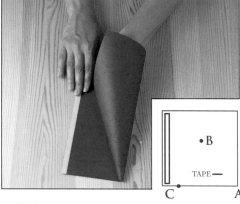

2 Take corner A (see inset) and curl it under to touch point B; point C shows where the narrow end begins. Continue curling until you have a cone; do not worry if the end is not pointed.

3 Remove the backing from the tape and stick the paper in place. At the bottom of the cone, turn a double fold to make sure that it is secured. Use double-sided tape or a staple to hold it.

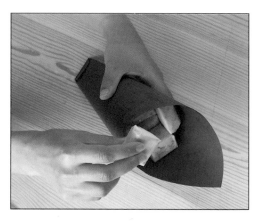

4 Fill the cone with the individually wrapped nougat pieces. Do not pack in so many that the cone bulges and loses its shape.

5 Fold in about 2.5 cm (1 in) at the front of the cone.

6 Fold the flap over and crease it horizontally at the back and front. Ease up the sides and crease to make triangular shapes, as if wrapping a box. Stick the side flaps to the cone using double-sided tape. It may be useful to practise folding a piece of scrap paper first.

7 Fold the string in half and tie a knot in the centre. You could also use ribbon that matches the paper.

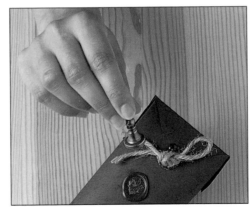

8 Scrape off small pieces of sealing wax with the knife and put them in the scoop. Heat the wax over a match flame until it melts. Immediately pour the wax in a small pool on to the point of the flap, and press on the string.

9 Melt a little more wax and pour one or more additional pools on to the cone to decorate it. Press on the seal or the coin. For a personalised gift, use a monogram seal. ✤

Note

Try making cones in a variety of colours and give a different one to each member of the family – a cornucopia of cones. You could also change the selection of sweets to suit the recipient.

SUGAR 'N' SPICE PECANS

PECAN HALVES ARE CANDIED IN LIGHTLY SPICED ORANGE SYRUP and packed
in a preserve jar with easy-to-make embossed tin foil plaques for labels.

RECIPE INGREDIENTS

375 g (12 oz) soft light brown sugar

250 ml (½ pint) orange juice

60 g (2 oz) lightly salted butter

Grated rind of 1 orange

1 teaspoon mild curry powder

Large pinch ground cayenne pepper

250 g (8 oz) pecan halves

The sugared nuts will fill one
625 g (1¼ lb) jar

PACKAGING NEEDS

*Soft pencil, tracing paper, scissors,
double-sided tape, all-purpose glue,
hole punch*

625 g (1¼ lb) preserving jar

*20 cm (8 in) foil baking case, to make
the jar label and gift tag*

Small piece of craft paper, for gift tag

Several sheets A4 paper

*½ m (½ yd) silver metallic ribbon,
3 mm (⅛ in) wide*

*1 m (1 yd) silky ribbon,
2.5 cm (1 in) wide*

RECIPE: Sugar 'n' spice pecans

Line a baking tray with greaseproof paper, or brush it lightly with oil.

1 In a medium-sized saucepan set over a low heat, stir the **sugar** and **orange juice** with a wooden spoon until the sugar has dissolved.

2 Turn up the heat, bring the syrup to the boil and boil without stirring until it reaches 116°C (240°F) on a sugar thermometer.

3 To test the temperature of the syrup without a thermometer, drop a small amount into a bowl or cup of iced water. If you can shape the sticky syrup into a soft ball that flattens when gently pressed with a finger, it is ready.

4 As soon as the syrup reaches this soft ball stage, remove the saucepan from the heat. Stir in the **butter, orange rind** and **spices** until well blended. Add the **pecans** and stir until they are well coated and begin to look sugary. ▶

5 Turn the mixture out of the saucepan on to the prepared baking tray. Using two forks, and working quickly, pull the nuts apart to separate them.

6 Place a piece of greaseproof paper on a wire rack. Transfer individual nuts to the paper, using a fork, and leave them in a dry place to harden overnight. Pack them into an airtight jar until you are ready to wrap them. ▪

GIFTWRAP: Making a good impression

Present this irresistibly spicy snack in style. The labels are cut from a foil baking case and embossed with the recipient's name.

1 Trace the design for the 'pecans' label from the pattern opposite on a piece of tracing paper, using a pencil.

2 Cut two pieces from the flat part of the foil baking case, one for the jar label, the other for the gift tag.

3 Place one piece of foil on several sheets of paper to make a soft surface. Put the 'pecans' tracing on it, so that the type is reversed. With a soft, blunt pencil, go over the outlines to emboss the pattern on the foil.

4 Emboss the outline of the leaf and nut design on to the other piece of foil. Then, following the outlines of the reversed alphabet opposite, write the name of the recipient on a piece of tracing paper. With the type back to front, emboss the name in the centre of the panel as before.

5 Cut out the embossed designs. Cut a piece of the silky ribbon 38 cm (15 in) long, to fit around the jar. Stick the 'pecans' label in the middle. Wrap the ribbon around the jar, with the label at the front. Fold in the ribbon edges at the back and stick them to the glass with double-sided tape.

6 Glue the name tag to the craft paper. Cut around the tag, leaving a margin of 3 mm (⅛ in) so that the paper is just visible.

7 Punch a hole at one end of the name tag and loop the metallic ribbon through it.

8 Coil the remaining silky ribbon inside the jar and arrange the pecans between the folds.

9 Thread the metallic ribbon through the fastening on the jar and tie on the gift tag. ✤

SUGAR-PASTE LEAVES

DECORATE A TERRACOTTA POT with trailing ivy and fill it with multicoloured edible leaves for an attractive and down-to-earth gift.

RECIPE INGREDIENTS

250g (8oz) granulated sugar

75ml (2½ fl oz) water

15g (½ oz) powdered glucose

*Orange, yellow and green edible
food colourings*

*Orange, vanilla and
peppermint essences*

Icing sugar, sifted, for dusting

*Small leaf-shaped confectionery
or biscuit cutters*

Makes 250g (8oz) leaves

PACKAGING NEEDS

*Pencil, tracing paper, craft knife, cutting
mat, masking tape, scissors, scrap
of cardboard, elastic band*

Stencil with trailing leaf design (page 80)

*Earthenware flowerpot, about 10cm (4in)
in diameter*

Green and brown dry-brush stencil paints

Stencil brush

*Piece of cellophane 20 by 20cm
(8 by 8in)*

*Cotton table napkin, about 50 by 50cm
(20 by 20in)*

*1m (1yd) wire-edged ribbon,
7.5cm (3in) wide, in a
contrasting colour*

RECIPE: Sugar-paste leaves

1 Put the **sugar** and **water** into a pan and dissolve over low heat, stirring with a long-handled metal spoon. Bring to the boil and stir in the **glucose.** Boil without stirring until the syrup reaches 116°C (240°F) on a sugar thermometer (see page 75, step 3 for the soft-ball test).

3 Using a spatula, 'work' the sugar paste by turning it over, forwards and backwards, in a figure-of-eight movement. When the paste is opaque, gather it into a ball and knead it until it is smooth. Set it aside to cool completely.

2 Brush a little cold water over a large cold surface, such as a marble slab or chopping board, and pour on the syrup. Let it cool for about 3 to 5 minutes until a skin begins to form around the edges.

4 Divide the paste into three. Using a skewer, colour each one with 2 to 3 drops of **food colouring** and add the appropriate **essence**. Knead each portion until the colouring and flavouring are well blended. ▶

5 Dust the work surface very lightly with sifted **icing sugar** and roll out each portion of paste to a thickness of 6 mm (¼ in). Cut out leaf shapes, using small confectionery or biscuit cutters. Gather up the trimmings in each separate colour, roll them out again and cut out more shapes.

6 Using a sharp knife, mark lines on the shapes to represent leaf veins. Arrange the finished leaves in a single layer on a wire rack and leave them in a warm place, such as an airing cupboard, to dry overnight. ⬛

GIFTWRAP: Gathering the harvest

Create a combined gift for the kitchen window sill and breakfast table by enclosing an earthenware pot of edible leaves in a two-tone cotton table napkin.

1 Draw around the outline of the stencil below on tracing paper and use a craft knife to cut it out. Attach masking tape to the stencil and position it on the pot so that the leaf pattern winds around it.

2 Mix the two colours of dry-brush paint on the scrap of cardboard to make varying shades. Then, working with one colour at a time, stencil the leaf design on the pot.

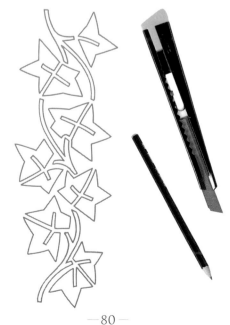

3 Reposition the stencil so that the leaves continue to wind around the pot. Continue stencilling the outline, then set the pot aside and let the paint dry thoroughly.

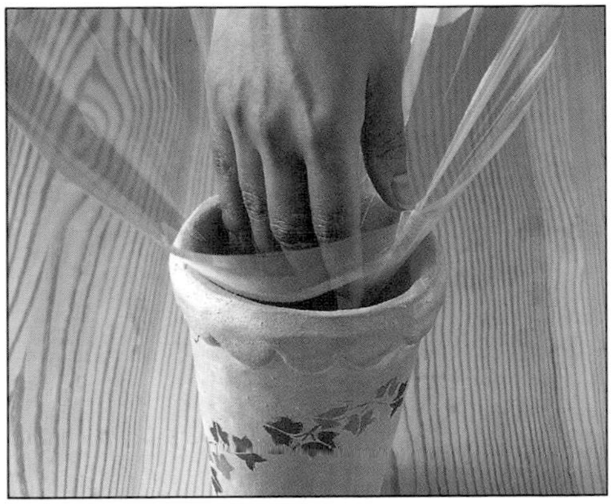

4 To prevent the sugar-paste leaves from touching the inside of the flowerpot, push the square of cellophane into the pot.

5 Fill the pot with the edible leaves. Draw the corners of the cellophane over the top.

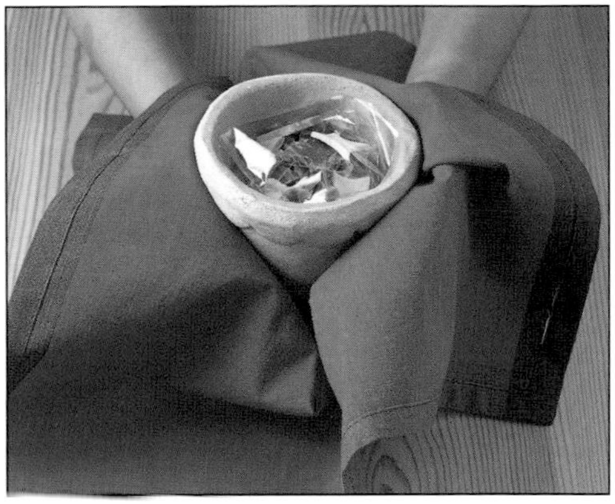

6 Place the napkin right side down on the work surface, stand the flowerpot in the centre and bring the four corners over the top to enclose the pot. Secure with an elastic band.

7 Tie the ribbon around the elastic band to hide it, and make a bow. Trim the ribbon ends neatly with a pair of scissors.

Note

In place of a flowerpot, you could pack the sugar-paste leaves into an airtight container or preserving jar before wrapping it in a cotton table napkin. For an even simpler gift, you could omit the wrapping altogether and decorate the container with a dried seed pod (above).

SUGAR-FROSTED FRUITS

FIRM, JUST-RIPE FRUITS, with contrasting colours, flavours and textures,
are presented in a decorative giant matchbox.

RECIPE INGREDIENTS

About 375 g (12 oz) mixed fresh fruits, such as kumquats, grapes, cherries, raspberries, blackberries, red currants, Cape gooseberries and small strawberries

1 large egg white

90 g (3 oz) caster sugar

Cocktail sticks or skewers, to hold stemless fruits

Frosts about 375 g (12 oz) small fruits

PACKAGING NEEDS

Ruler, pencil, craft knife, cutting mat, scissors, double-sided tape

Piece of medium-weight cardboard 17.3 by 29.8 cm (6¾ by 11⅝ in), for the box

Piece of thin cardboard 20 by 31 cm (7⅞ by 12¼ in), for the sliding cover

Piece of wrapping paper 24 by 31 cm (9⅜ by 12¼ in), to cover the sliding cover

Small confectionery cases

About ¾ m (¾ yd) wire-edged ribbon, 5 cm (2 in) wide

RECIPE: Sugar-frosted fruits

1 Rinse the **fruits** under cold running water, taking care not to bruise them. Keep the stems on if possible for more attractive presentation, and retain the papery Cape gooseberry cases. Dry the fruits gently on paper towel.

3 In a small bowl, lightly beat the **egg white** using a wire whisk. Place the **sugar** in a larger bowl.

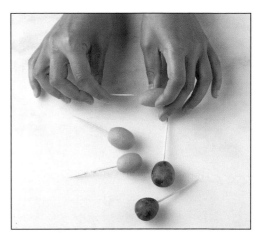

2 Using a cocktail stick or fine skewer, carefully pierce each piece of fruit that does not have a stem.

4 One by one, dip the pieces of fruit in the egg white to coat them and shake off the excess. Hold the fruit by the cocktail stick or stem, as applicable. ▶

5 Dip the egg-white coated fruit in the sugar, turning it to cover the fruit completely. Use a teaspoon, if necessary, to sprinkle sugar over any parts that remain uncovered.

6 Place the fruit on a wire rack in a warm, dry place, such as an airing cupboard, and leave to dry for several hours or overnight. When dry, carefully remove the cocktail sticks. ▪▪

GIFTWRAP: A fruitful package

An outsize matchbox covered in bright giftwrap, this sliding box can be used to present many other sweet things, too. (See page 126 for templates of box and sliding cover.)

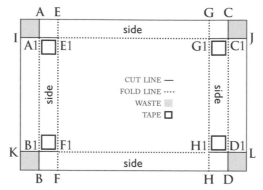

1 To make the box, use the medium-weight cardboard. Follow the template (left) and use a craft knife to score (not cut) lines A-B and C-D, each 2 cm (¾ in) in from and parallel to the short sides. Then score lines E-F and G-H, each 2.9 cm (1⅛ in) in from and parallel to those lines. Score lines I-J and K-L, each 2.9 cm (1⅛ in) in from and parallel to the long sides.

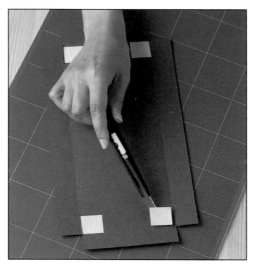

2 Using a craft knife, cut away the rectangles at the four corners, and cut through the lines A1-E1, C1-G1, D1-H1 and B1-F1. Stick 2.5 cm (1 in) squares of double-sided tape where indicated by the bold outlines on the template.

3 Peel the backing from the tape, fold up the long sides of the box and press the corner flaps to the tape. Fold over the two narrow end sections, I-A1-B1-K and J-C1-D1-L.

4 To make the sliding cover, score a line 1.5 cm (½ in) from and parallel to one of the short sides of the thinner card. Then score another line a further 3 cm (1¼ in) along, another a further 11.75 cm (4⅝ in) and another a further 3 cm (1¼ in) along. This last line will be 11.75 cm (4⅝ in) in from the opposite edge.

5 Cover the entire back of the wrapping paper from edge to edge with strips of double-sided tape and trim the ends, using the craft knife.

6 With the double-sided tape facing up, measure and mark a spot 2 cm (¾ in) in from each of the long edges at both ends. Peel off the backing strips and, using the marked spots as a guide, place the cardboard, scored side up, so that the short edges of the cardboard and paper align.

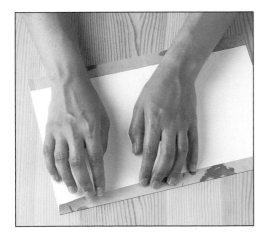

7 Press the cardboard down firmly on to the wrapping paper and fold the excess paper over the cardboard.

8 Bend the cardboard along the scored lines and secure the overlap with double-sided tape or glue.

9 Arrange the confectionery cases in the box and put a piece of frosted fruit in each one. Slide the cover over the box and tie the ribbon into a bow around it. Trim the ribbon ends neatly. ❧

Cakes & Desserts

🎁 A CAKE CAN MAKE AN OCCASION. Express the spirit of the holiday season with Thanksgiving pumpkin pie or rich Christmas fruitcake baked in a round mould. For Valentine's day, offer frosted rose-petal cake, light-as-air cake or four-layer spice cake with a sugar and cinnamon bow. Old-fashioned gingerbread is given a lift with edible gold leaf; cocoa and glacé fruits ring the changes in an Italian fruitcake; and no one will be able to resist chocolate-pecan gateau or butterscotch-topped cheesecake.

Ready-made boxes are a feature here: painted with a crackle finish, adorned with pressed leaves and covered with floral paper. A wooden sieve and an open-weave basket are also pressed into service. Sweet wrappers brighten tissue paper, and flamboyant bows are the accent on a homemade box and a simple fabric package. And presenting your dessert on a beautiful plate will save your hostess time, as well as being a lasting gift.

ROSE-PETAL CAKE

FLAVOURED WITH ROSEWATER AND SCENTED ROSE PETALS and decorated with sugar-frosted petals, this cake sets the scene for an elegant and romantic rendezvous.

RECIPE INGREDIENTS

125 g (4 oz) lightly salted butter, softened

125 g (4 oz) caster sugar

2 large eggs, separated

125 g (4 oz) plain flour

1 tablespoon (15 ml) rosewater

About 12 fragrant rose petals, rinsed
and patted dry

ICING

1-2 teaspoons (5-10 ml) rosewater

125 g (4 oz) icing sugar, sifted

Makes one 18 cm (7 in) cake

PACKAGING NEEDS

Hairdryer, greaseproof
paper, all-purpose glue, scissors

Round wooden, cardboard or papier-mâché
box and lid 20 cm (8 in) in diameter and at
least 9 cm (3½ in) deep

Vinyl matt water-based paints in two
contrasting shades of pink

1.5 cm (½ in) paintbrush

Clear water-based satin varnish

Small piece of sponge

3 small containers, such as foil tart tins

Tissue paper

DECORATION FOR CAKE AND BOX

2 large egg whites, lightly beaten

3 heaped tablespoons caster sugar

Individual rose petals, rinsed and
patted dry, for the cake

2 or 3 pink rosebuds, slightly open,
for the box

60 cm (24 in) gossamer ribbon,
4 cm (1½ in) wide

RECIPE: Rose-petal cake

Preheat the oven to 180°C (350°F/Gas 4). Lightly brush an 18 cm (7 in) cake tin with oil or melted butter and dust it with flour, tipping out any excess flour.

1 In a mixing bowl, cream the **butter** and **sugar** together until they are light and fluffy, then beat in the **egg yolks** a little at a time.

2 In another bowl, beat the egg whites until stiff. Lightly fold them and the **flour** alternately into the butter mixture. Stir in the **rosewater.**

3 Line the bottom of the prepared cake tin with the **rose petals** and pour in the mixtures. (The petals impart a delicate rose flavour to the cake, but do not retain their colour when baked.)

4 Bake in the preheated oven for about 35 minutes, until the cake is lightly brown and feels springy to the touch. Leave the cake to cool in the tin for a few minutes before turning it out on to a wire rack to cool completely. ▶

5 To make the icing, stir just enough **rosewater** into the **icing sugar** to give a coating consistency. Spread it over the top and side of the cake using a palette knife.

6 To make the frosted rose petals for decoration, see steps 6 and 7 on page 91. Arrange the rose petals on the cake, using a little more icing to attach them if the cake icing has already set. ▪▪

GIFTWRAP: Summer flowers

A papier-mâché box with a scalloped lid, painted in two shades of pink and trimmed with sugar-frosted roses, is as decorative as the cake it holds.

1 Pour a little of the darker pink paint into one of the containers and paint the base and sides of the box, brushing the paint on in one direction only. Wash the paintbrush.

2 Pour a little of the varnish into a container and, working quickly, while the pink paint is still wet, brush on the varnish.

3 Dry with the hairdryer until the varnish crackles, then leave the container to dry completely.

4 Pour a little of the contrasting paint into another container and make a pad with the sponge. Dip the sponge into the paint and rub it into the cracks all over the box.

5 Paint the lid in a similar way, but brush it with the paler colour first. While this is wet, apply the varnish, 'crackle' with the hairdryer, and when it is dry, rub in the darker colour.

6 To make the decoration for the cake and the box, put the lightly beaten **egg whites** in a shallow bowl and the **sugar** on a plate. One at a time, brush the **petals** and **rosebuds** with the egg, covering every surface. Allow any excess to drip back into the bowl.

7 Using a teaspoon, sprinkle the caster sugar over the petals and buds, making sure to cover all the surfaces. Place them on a sheet of greaseproof paper and leave in a warm place, such as an airing cupboard, to dry out for at least 3 hours.

8 When they are dry, tie the frosted roses into a bunch with the ribbon and glue them to the lid of the box. Trim the ribbon ends neatly with scissors.

9 Line the box with the tissue paper before putting in the cake. Carefully lower it into the box using a strip of greaseproof paper (see page 95, step 9). ❖

Note

You can frost the rose petals or rosebuds well in advance of making the cake. Once they are thoroughly dry, store them between layers of paper towel in an airtight container.

CHOCOLATE-PECAN GATEAU

MADE WITH GROUND PECANS AND WITHOUT ANY FLOUR, this rich, sumptuous cake has a glossy chocolate topping, decorated with chocolate-coated nuts.

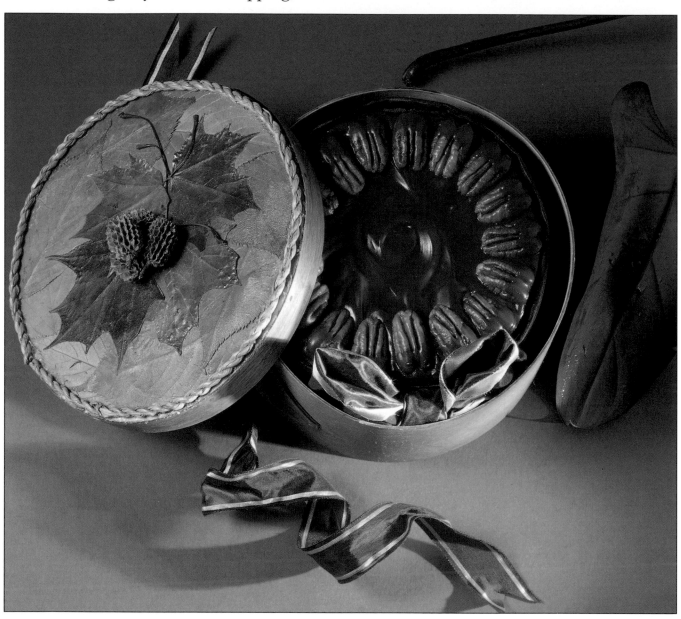

RECIPE INGREDIENTS

175g (6oz) plain chocolate

90g (3oz) lightly salted butter

60g (2oz) caster sugar

3 large eggs

1 teaspoon (5ml) vanilla essence

90g (3oz) pecans, ground

About 20 pecan halves

ICING

2 tablespoons (30ml) clear honey

45g (1½oz) lightly salted butter

90g (3oz) plain chocolate

Makes one 15 cm (6 in) cake

PACKAGING NEEDS

Colourless wax furniture polish, soft polishing cloth, all-purpose glue, scissors, greaseproof paper, double-sided tape

Wooden or cardboard box with lid, at least 16.5 cm (6½ in) in diameter and 7.5 cm (3 in) deep

Medium-brown wood stain

2 cm (¾ in) paintbrush

Selection of golden fallen leaves, pressed (see Note page 95)

Thick string, at least 54 cm (21 in) long

Matt polyurethane varnish

3 to 6 small pine cones

¾ m (¾ yd) silk ribbon, 6.5 cm (2½ in) wide

RECIPE: Chocolate-pecan gateau

Preheat the oven to 180°C (350°F/Gas 4). Line a 15 cm (6 in) round cake tin with greaseproof paper.

1 Place the **chocolate,** broken in pieces, and **butter** in a saucepan over a low heat. Stir occasionally until the mixture has melted, then remove it from the heat and let it cool slightly.

2 Beat the **sugar, eggs** and **vanilla essence,** preferably with an electric mixer, until the mixture is pale and creamy. Using a metal spoon, fold in the chocolate mixture and ground **nuts** until the mixture is well blended.

3 Pour the mixture into the prepared tin and smooth the top. Bake in the preheated oven for 30 to 35 minutes, until the cake feels springy to the touch. Stand the tin on a wire rack to cool. Turn the cake out when cool.

4 To make the icing, melt the **honey, butter** and **chocolate** in a small bowl set over a saucepan of simmering water, stirring occasionally. ▶

GIFTWRAP: A patchwork of leaves

A wooden box covered with golden pressed leaves contains an earthy, chocolaty cake, perfect for shortening autumnal days.

5 Lift the bowl off the saucepan and dip the pecan halves into the mixture to half-coat them. Place the nuts on greaseproof paper to dry.

1 Following directions on the product, brush stain evenly over the side and base of the box and the side of the lid. Leave it to dry and apply another coat if you wish.

2 When the stain is dry, rub the treated areas with furniture polish.

6 Turn the cake upside-down and remove the paper. Spread the icing over the top of the cake only, using a spatula dipped in hot water. Arrange the nuts around the edge. Store the cake in an airtight container once the icing sets. ▪

3 Spread a thin coat of glue over the outer edge of the box lid. Arrange pressed leaves around the rim, spreading glue thinly over leaves where they overlap.

4 With the scissors, carefully cut close to the edge of the lid, trimming off the parts of any leaves that hang over the edge of the rim.

5 Complete the patchwork of leaves, then glue the string around the outside edge of the lid to protect the cut edges of the leaves. Brush the leaves with varnish and set aside to dry.

6 Arrange a cluster of cones in the centre of the lid to see how they look. When you are happy with the combination, glue them in place.

7 Cut a 50 by 6.5 cm (20 by 2½ in) strip of greaseproof paper. Wrap the band around the cake and seal the seam with double-sided tape.

8 Cut off a 50 cm (20 in) length of ribbon and turn under the two edges to hide them. Stick a strip of double-sided tape vertically down the paper band. Wrap the ribbon around the cake and stick down the ends. Tie a small bow with the remaining ribbon and attach it to the band with tape to cover the seam.

9 Line the box with a circle of greaseproof paper. Place the cake on a strip of greaseproof paper and gently lower it into the box. Carefully slide the paper out from under the cake. 🎁

Note

Gather a selection of leaves to press in the autumn, since their colours come up well when dried. Dust the leaves and pat off any dampness with paper towel. Arrange them in a single layer between sheets of paper and place them in a large book such as a telephone directory. Put more books or weights on top. The leaves should be dry and pressed flat in 2 to 3 weeks.

OLD-FASHIONED GINGERBREAD

UNWRAP THE GIANT SWEET TO REVEAL A MOIST GINGERBREAD, full of candied ginger
and topped with edible gold leaf, which keeps well and even improves with time.

RECIPE INGREDIENTS

175 g (6 oz) plain flour

2 teaspoons ground ginger

½ teaspoon ground cinnamon

¼ teaspoon grated nutmeg

Pinch salt

90 g (3 oz) candied ginger, finely chopped

125 g (4 oz) black treacle

60 g (2 oz) lightly salted butter

90 g (3 oz) soft dark brown sugar

1 large egg, lightly beaten

3 tablespoons (45 ml) milk

½ teaspoon bicarbonate of soda

DECORATION

2 tablespoons (30 ml) honey

Edible gold leaf

Makes one 500 g (1 lb) cake

PACKAGING NEEDS

Foil, tracing or greaseproof paper, scissors, tape, paper glue

1 sheet tissue paper

New 500 g (1 lb) loaf tin

Foil sweet wrappers, or pieces of gold, silver and coloured foil wrapping

Double-sided tape, 8 mm (³⁄₈ in) wide

½ m (½ yd) each of 2 colours of satin ribbon, 3 mm (⅛ in) wide

RECIPE: Old-fashioned gingerbread

Preheat the oven to 180°C (350°F/Gas 4). Line a 500 g (1 lb) loaf tin with greaseproof paper.

1 Sift the **flour, spices** and **salt** into a mixing bowl. Stir in the chopped **ginger.** In a small saucepan, over a low heat, melt the **treacle, butter** and **sugar** stirring occasionally.

2 Gradually pour the melted sugar mixture into the dry ingredients and stir well with a wooden spoon. Beat in the **egg.**

3 Put the **milk** into a cup and sprinkle the **bicarbonate of soda** on to it. Stir well and then stir it into the mixture in the bowl.

4 Pour the mixture into the prepared tin and smooth the top. Bake in the preheated oven for 40 to 45 minutes. To test if baked through, insert a skewer into the middle; it should come out clean. ▶

5 Stand the tin on a wire rack and leave the gingerbread to cool slightly before turning it out. Melt the **honey** and brush it over the top of the cake while it is still warm.

6 Tear off small pieces of **gold leaf** and press them on to the cake, using a small craft brush. When the cake is cool, wrap it tightly in foil and store it an airtight container until you are ready to wrap it. ▪▪

GIFTWRAP: A gingerbread cracker

Give a sparkling new baking tin as part of the gift – particularly apt for a keen cook – so the recipient can make the gingerbread again and again.

1 If necessary, remove the old foil from the cake and rewrap the gingerbread tightly in a fresh piece of foil.

3 Carefully place the wrapped cake in the new loaf tin. The wrapping may create a snug fit.

2 Overwrap the cake in tracing paper, sticking down the edges neatly with tape.

4 Prepare the sweet wrappers or pieces of foil wrapping by gently smoothing out the foil, using your thumbnail.

5 With the tissue paper right side up, place the tin in the centre of the paper and place a length of string or ribbon around the outside of it. Then glue sweet wrappers or scraps of coloured foil around the outside of the string or ribbon, using dabs of glue.

6 Continue sticking on sweet wrappers, placing them at random to give a patchwork effect. You will need to glue all around the outline, so that the sides and top of the tin are covered when it is wrapped.

7 Place the tissue paper right side down on the work surface. Position the cake tin in the centre of the paper, checking to see that it sits on the undecorated area. Fold over the long sides of the paper to make a neat edge.

8 Bring the long sides of the paper up over the tin and make a pleated fold so that the sweet wrappers meet in the middle. Use some double-sided tape to secure the parcel.

9 To make the ends of the parcel, carefully pinch in the tissue paper, taking care not to tear it. Cut the ribbons in half. Tie them around each end of the parcel, forming a bow. Trim the ends of the tissue paper and open them out. 🎁

Note

For a simpler look, or if you are pressed for time, you may prefer to wrap the gingerbread in its tin in undecorated tissue paper. Tie the two ribbons crosswise around the parcel. Alternatively, you could add a flamboyant ready-made bow.

BUTTERSCOTCH-TOPPED CHEESECAKE

THE ATTRACTIVE PRESENTATION OF THIS CHEESECAKE on a decorative plate, not to mention the buttery smooth taste, makes it an ideal gift for a dinner party.

RECIPE INGREDIENTS

BASE

75 g (2½ oz) lightly salted butter

125 g (4 oz) gingernuts, crushed

FILLING

2 tablespoons seedless raisins

2 tablespoons (30 ml) sweet sherry or brandy

250 g (8 oz) cream cheese

125 g (4 oz) curd cheese

2 large eggs

125 g (4 oz) caster sugar

30 g (1 oz) plain flour

150 ml (¼ pint) crème fraîche or soured cream

Grated rind of 1 orange

2 tablespoons (30 ml) orange juice

BUTTERSCOTCH TOPPING

175 g (6 oz) can full-cream sweetened condensed milk

60 g (2 oz) caster sugar

90 g (3 oz) lightly salted butter

2 tablespoons (30 ml) honey

PACKAGING NEEDS

Tape, scissors, elastic band

Strip of greaseproof paper, about 6.5 by 63 cm (2½ by 25 in)

About 76 cm (30 in) grosgrain ribbon, 2.5 cm (1 in) wide

About 25 dried bay leaves

About 13 kumquats

Dinner plate or serving plate with a 20 cm (8 in) flat centre

Clear cellophane, about 1 m (1 yd) square

15 cm (6 in) satin ribbon, 7.5 cm (3 in) wide

25 cm (10 in) medium-gauge flexible wire

Cocktail stick

RECIPE: Butterscotch-topped cheesecake

Preheat the oven to 180°C (350°F/Gas 4). Lightly brush a 20 cm (8 in) springform cake tin with vegetable oil.

1 Melt the **butter** in a small saucepan, then stir in the crushed **gingernuts**. Turn the mixture into the cake tin and press it with the back of a spoon to cover the bottom. Set aside while you make the filling.

2 Soak the **raisins** in the **sherry** and set aside. Using a wire whisk, beat together the **cheeses** and **eggs** in a mixing bowl, then beat in the **sugar**.

3 Fold in the **flour** and the **crème fraîche** with a metal spoon. Stir in the raisins and sherry, the **orange rind** and **orange juice**.

4 Pour the mixture into the tin, level the top and bake in the preheated oven for 45 minutes, or until a skewer inserted into the centre comes out clean. Stand on a wire rack to cool completely. ▶

5 For the topping, put the **condensed milk, sugar, butter** and **honey** into a saucepan and stir over a low heat until they melt. Bring to the boil, and boil for 3 minutes without stirring.

6 Immediately pour the butterscotch mixture over the cheesecake and set it aside to cool. Wrap the cheesecake, still in the tin, in foil and store it in the refrigerator until you are ready to giftwrap it. ▪▪

GIFTWRAP: Presentation plate

You might like to get together with other guests going to a party and take your buffet gifts on a set of matching plates.

1 Remove the cheesecake from the cake tin, wrap the greaseproof paper strip around the side and join the edges with tape.

2 Cut 63 cm (25 in) of the grosgrain ribbon and wrap it around the cheesecake. Tape the seam; if you wish, you can add a bow to hide the join.

3 Arrange the bay leaves around the cheesecake, between the paper and the ribbon band. Place a kumquat in the centre and add two more bay leaves.

4 Place the plate in the centre of the square of cellophane. Using a fish slice, carefully place the cheesecake in the centre of the plate.

5 Draw the corners of the cellophane over the top of the cake and use an elastic band to hold them in place.

6 Tie the piece of wide satin ribbon over the elastic band to hide it. Tuck in the ends of the ribbon so that they do not show.

7 Thread the kumquats on to the medium-gauge wire. It may help if you make a hole with a cocktail stick in each fruit first so that you can arrange them neatly on the wire.

8 Wrap the kumquat-covered wire around the top of the parcel, just below the ribbon, and twist the ends of the wire to secure the ring. If necessary, trim off any extra wire.

9 Once the kumquat ring is in place, arrange the cellophane by teasing out the top of the parcel with your fingers. 🎁

Note

If you present the cheesecake on a less decorative plate and do not have far to travel, you could omit the cellophane wrapping and make a larger kumquat ring to form a border around the dessert.

ITALIAN CHOCOLATE FRUITCAKE

COMBINING NUTS, EXOTIC GLACÉ FRUITS AND COCOA, this chewy Italian panforte
has something to appeal to all palates.

RECIPE INGREDIENTS

125 g (4 oz) blanched almonds, chopped, plus 4 whole ones for decoration

125 g (4 oz) hazelnuts, chopped

60 g (2 oz) pecan halves, chopped

60 g (2 oz) dried figs, chopped

250 g (8 oz) mixed glacé fruits, such as pineapple, apricots, citron and pears, chopped

60 g (2 oz) plain flour

30 g (1 oz) cocoa powder, sifted

1 teaspoon ground cinnamon, plus extra for dusting

¼ teaspoon ground cloves

125 g (4 oz) granulated sugar

125 g (4 oz) clear honey

1 teaspoon (5 ml) rosewater

2 tablespoons icing sugar, sifted, for dusting

Makes one 20 cm (8 in) cake

PACKAGING NEEDS

Scissors, masking tape, rubber gloves, ruler, pencil, elastic band

A shallow woven basket with a handle, at least 21.5 by 21.5 cm (8½ by 8½ in)

Mauve and pink emulsion paints or acrylic water-based paints

2 small containers, such as foil tart tins

Medium-grade wire wool

1.5 cm (½ in) paintbrush

Sheet of parchment paper

Calligraphy pen and ink

1 m (1 yd) cotton ribbon, 1.5 cm (½ in) wide

Tissue paper, to line basket

RECIPE: Italian chocolate fruitcake

Preheat the oven to 180°C (350°F/Gas 4). Line the bottom and sides of a 20 cm (8 in) square baking tin with greaseproof paper.

1 Spread the chopped **almonds** and **hazelnuts** on a baking tray and toast them in the preheated oven for 5 to 6 minutes, stirring them once or twice, until they are brown. Leave them to cool slightly.

2 In a mixing bowl, stir together the toasted chopped almonds and hazelnuts, the **pecans** and the chopped **figs** and other **fruits.**

3 Sift in the **flour, cocoa powder, cinnamon** and **cloves** and stir the ingredients well.

4 Heat the **sugar** and **honey** in a saucepan over a low heat until the sugar melts. Pour the syrup into the dry ingredients, add the **rosewater** and mix well. ▶

5 Spoon the mixture into the prepared tin and press it into the corners with a wooden spoon. Bake in the preheated oven for 35 to 40 minutes, until a skewer inserted in the centre of the cake comes out clean.

6 Stand the tin on a wire rack to cool, then turn out the cake and peel off the paper. Sift **icing sugar** over the top and decorate it with whole toasted almonds. (To store the cake, wrap it in foil and place it in an airtight container without dusting it with icing sugar.) ▪▪

GIFTWRAP: Carrying on the tradition

Presenting your gift with a scroll containing a handwritten copy of this centuries-old recipe will mean that it can be enjoyed for a long time to come.

1 Cut strips of masking tape and stick it around the rim of the basket and over the handle to protect these areas while you apply the mauve paint to the rest of the basket.

2 Pour a little of the mauve paint into a foil container. Put on the rubber gloves and tear off a piece of wire wool about 5 cm (2 in) square. Crumple it to make a workable pad.

3 Dip the pad into the paint and rub it on to the basket, working in the direction of the grain on each of the wood strips. Do not try to paint right into the edges of the squares; it makes a more interesting chequered effect if you do not.

4 When the paint is dry, peel off the masking tape from the rim and handle. Apply more tape around the top of the basket, just beneath the rim, to protect the painted area.

5 Pour a little of the pink paint into the second container. Using the brush, paint the rim and both sides of the handle. Leave the paint to dry, then peel off the tape.

6 Measure and cut a piece of the parchment paper about 20 by 25 cm (8 by 10 in), or to suit the size of your handwriting. Copy the recipe for the fruit cake, using a calligraphy pen and ink.

7 Cut off 60 cm (24 in) of the ribbon. To make a scroll, roll up the recipe, secure it with an elastic band, and tie the ribbon around it. Remove the band after the ribbon is tied into a bow.

8 To make a gift tag, cut a small piece of the parchment paper, write a message on it, roll it up and tie it to the handle of the basket with the remaining ribbon.

9 Place the tissue paper in the basket to line it and carefully put the cake on top of the paper. Trim the tissue paper with scissors and tuck in the edges so that they do not stick above the rim. Balance the recipe scroll across one corner of the basket. 🎁

Note

On the recipe scroll, you could include hints on how to serve the cake. Traditionally, it is cut into thin rectangular pieces and enjoyed with a cup of strong Italian coffee or a sweet fortified wine, such as Vin Santo.

FOUR-LAYER SPICE CAKE

THIS 'ANYTIME' CAKE, WITH ITS SUGAR AND CINNAMON BOW, can be served
with a cup of coffee or tea, or as a dessert.

RECIPE INGREDIENTS

125 g (4 oz) lightly salted butter, softened

175 g (6 oz) granulated sugar

125 g (4 oz) soft dark brown sugar

3 large eggs

125 ml (4 fl oz) milk

125 g (4 oz) molasses

300 g (10 oz) plain flour

1 teaspoon salt

½ teaspoon bicarbonate of soda

2 teaspoons ground cinnamon

¼ teaspoon each ground cloves and nutmeg

ICING AND DECORATION

125 g (4 oz) lightly salted butter

125 g (4 oz) molasses

3 tablespoons (45 ml) milk

175–250 g (6–8 oz) icing sugar

2 tablespoons caster sugar

1 teaspoon ground cinnamon

Bow-shaped stencil outline (page 127), plus thin piece of cardboard 20 by 20 cm (8 by 8 in)

Makes one 15 cm (6 in) cake

PACKAGING NEEDS

Ruler, soft pencil, craft knife, cutting mat, tape, double-sided tape, tracing paper

Wooden strainer 18 cm (7 in) in diameter, or a cardboard box at least 7.5 cm (3 in) deep

Piece of heavy cardboard 19 by 19 cm (7½ by 7½ in), for the lid

Piece of thin cardboard 5 by 61 cm (2 by 24 in), for the side of the lid

Piece of craft paper 26 by 61 cm (10½ by 24 in), to cover the lid

Emulsion paint or acrylic water-based paint

Small craft paintbrush

Gold craft powder

About 1.6 m (1¼ yd) ribbon, 6.5 cm (2½ in) wide

RECIPE: Four-layer spice cake

Preheat the oven to 180°C (350°F/Gas 4). Lightly brush two 15 cm (6 in) cake tins with oil and dust them with flour, shaking out the excess.

1 In a mixing bowl, cream the **butter** with a wooden spoon. Gradually beat in the **granulated** and **dark brown sugars** and beat until light and fluffy. Beat in the **eggs** one at a time.

2 Gradually beat in the **milk** and **molasses**. Sift together the **flour, salt, bicarbonate of soda, cinnamon, cloves** and **nutmeg**, then gradually add the dry ingredients to the butter mixture. Stir until well blended.

3 Pour the mixture into the prepared tins, level the tops and bake in the preheated oven for 40 to 45 minutes, until a skewer inserted into the middle comes out clean. Cool the cakes in the tins, then turn them out on to a wire rack to cool completely.

4 To make the icing, melt the **butter** and **molasses** in a saucepan over a low heat. Stir in the **milk** and mix well. Let the mixture cool, then sift in enough **icing sugar** to produce a thick, spreadable consistency. ▶

5 While the icing cools, cut each of the cake layers in half horizontally. Spread three of them with the frosting using a spatula dipped in hot water and sandwich them together.

6 Sift together the **caster sugar** and the remaining ground cinnamon. Place the bow-shaped stencil (see steps 6 and 7 opposite) on top of the cake and sift the spiced sugar over it. Carefully lift off the stencil, to preserve the crisp outlines of the decoration. ▪

GIFTWRAP: Tied up in bows

The cake is presented in a surprise gift box – a wooden strainer with a simple-to-make cardboard lid – decorated, like the cake itself, with a ribbon bow motif.

1 Make the lid following the general instructions for making the round box lid on pages 8–9.

3 Position the lid on the paper with the top 1.5 cm (½ in) from one side and the inside 6 mm (¼ in) from the other. Peel off the backing and press the strip firmly around the side of the lid, smoothing it as you go.

2 To cover the lid, measure the circumference of the lid and the depth plus 2 cm (¾ in). Cut a strip of craft paper this size. Here, the strip is 61 cm (24 in) long and 7 cm (2¾ in) wide. Cover the paper strip on the wrong side with double-sided tape.

4 Snip the paper at intervals around the overlapping edges to make folding easier. Fold over the two edges and press them firmly in place on the inside and the top of the lid.

5 Cut a circle of the craft paper to fit the top of the lid exactly. Cover the paper on the wrong side with strips of double-sided tape and trim the edges.

6 Trace the ribbon-and-bow outline on page 127 on to the tracing paper. Place the paper on a piece of cardboard and press hard over the design with a soft pencil.

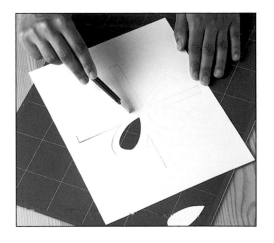

7 Using a craft knife on a cutting mat, cut out the bow shape from the cardboard. This will also be used as a stencil to make the 'ribbon' on the cake.

8 Place the bow-shaped stencil outline in the centre of the paper circle and draw around the shape with a pencil. Paint in the ribbon-and-bow shape. If the paper is absorbent, you might need to go over the shape again once the first coat has dried.

9 Peel off the backing strips from the double-sided tape and stick the paper circle to the lid. Brush the painted motif lightly with the gold craft powder.

10 Carefully lower the cake into the strainer (see page 95, step 9), taking care not to damage the sugar bow. Carefully tuck in about 40 cm (16 in) of the ribbon around the cake, between the cake and the strainer. Put the lid on the strainer. Wrap the remaining ribbon around the package and tie a bow. Trim the ends neatly. ✦

THANKSGIVING PUMPKIN PIE

PUMPKIN AND PECANS COMBINE TO MAKE A RICH, CRUNCHY PIE
that is the perfect end to any festive meal.

RECIPE INGREDIENTS

175 g (6 oz) plain flour

2 teaspoons caster sugar

½ teaspoon salt

2 teaspoons grated orange rind

90 g (3 oz) cold unsalted butter

1 large egg yolk

3 tablespoons (45 ml) double cream

FILLING

500 g (1 lb) pumpkin, peeled, seeded and cubed (prepared weight)

2 large eggs, lightly beaten

90 g (3 oz) light brown sugar

2 teaspoons ground cinnamon

1 teaspoon ground ginger

½ teaspoon salt

3 tablespoons (45 ml) molasses

4 tablespoons (60 ml) double cream

2 tablespoons (30 ml) orange juice

125 g (4 oz) pecan halves

Milk, for brushing

Icing sugar, sifted, for dusting

PACKAGING NEEDS

Ruler, pencil, craft knife, cutting mat, double-sided tape, scissors, tape, all-purpose glue, tracing or greaseproof paper

Piece of stiff cardboard 35 by 35 cm (14 by 14 in), for the box

Piece of stiff cardboard 32 by 32 cm (12¾ by 12¾ in), for the lid

Piece of craft paper 40 by 40 cm (16 by 16 in), to cover the box

Piece of coordinating craft paper 37 by 37 cm (14¾ by 14¾ in), to cover the lid

2 m (2 yd) gossamer ribbon, 5 cm (2 in) wide

Tissue paper

RECIPE: Thanksgiving pumpkin pie
Preheat the oven to 200°C (400°F/Gas 6). Grease a 23 cm (9 in) pie tin.

1 To make the pie crust, sift the **flour, sugar** and **salt** into a bowl and stir in the **orange rind.** Using your fingertips, rub in the **butter** until the mixture resembles fine crumbs. Beat the **egg yolk** and **cream** together in a small bowl, then stir into the dry ingredients.

2 Combine everything into a dough and shape it into a ball. Turn the dough on to a lightly floured surface and knead it until it is smooth. Wrap the dough in clingfilm and chill it in the refrigerator for at least 30 minutes.

3 To make the filling, steam the **pumpkin** cubes over a saucepan of simmering water for about 5 minutes, or until tender. Set aside to cool.

4 In a mixing bowl, mash the pumpkin with a potato masher or fork, then stir in the beaten **eggs, brown sugar, spices, salt** and **molasses.** Beat in the **cream** and **orange juice.** ▶

GIFTWRAP: Spice-box special

Cinnamon-coloured ribbon wrapped around the lid and tied into a filmy bow decorates a box covered in two-tone textured papers.

5 Roll out the pastry to line the pie tin, trim the edge and prick the bottom with a fork. Cover the pastry with greaseproof paper and bake blind in the preheated oven for 15 minutes. Reroll the trimmings and cut them into stars.

6 Pour the filling into the pie shell and arrange the **pecans** on top. Brush the pastry edge with **milk** and arrange the stars around it. Bake in the preheated oven for 45 to 50 minutes, until a skewer inserted in the middle comes out clean. Cool on a wire rack before removing from the tin. ▪▪

1 Using the instructions for a square box on pages 6–7, make the box.

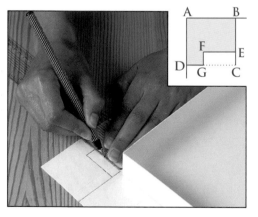

3 Place the lid in the centre of the wrong side of the paper. Using the template inset, from one corner, A, measure and mark a square up to the edge of the box, with points B, C and D. Mark point G on the line D-C so that G-C is equal to the width of the lid sides, then draw in line F-E parallel to G-C and 2 cm (¾ in) from it.

2 Cut strips of double-sided tape and completely cover the back of both pieces of craft paper.

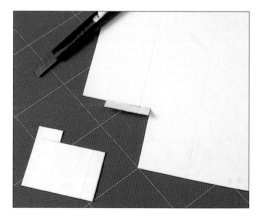

4 Cut along the line B-E-F-G-D using a craft knife on a cutting mat, and remove the corner section. Cut along the line E-C and fold the line G-C. Repeat this cut-and-fold sequence at the other three corners.

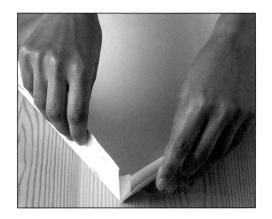

5 Practise folding the paper before removing the tape backing. Place the lid in the centre of the paper. At each corner, fold up the side with the flap and bend the flap at right angles. Fold up the other side to cover the flap, and fold in the overlap on both sides to the inside of the box.

6 To cover the lid with the paper, peel the backing strip from the tape, place the lid in the centre of the paper and press down on the base to make sure the paper is stuck. Then make the folds (see step 5) and secure.

7 Cover the box with coordinating paper in a similar way, placing the box in the centre of the paper, marking and cutting away the corner sections to make neat folds. Check that distance G-C is the width of the side of the box.

8 Cut the ribbon in half and cut a 38 cm (15 in) length from one piece. Wrap that around the lid about 5 cm (2 in) from one side, fold the two ends under and anchor them to the inside of the lid with tape.

9 Place the shorter length of the remaining ribbon on top of the longer one, with the centres together. Tie the two thicknesses together into a bow (it may help to have something to tie around, such as a pencil). Trim the ends and glue the bow to the ribbon band on the lid.

10 Cut a piece of tracing paper to line the box. Dust the edge of the pie with icing sugar, then put it in the box. Place crumpled tissue paper in each corner. 🎁

LIGHT-AS-AIR CAKE

CUTTING INTO THIS DELICIOUS CAKE reveals its inner strawberries-and-cream colouring, perfect for a birthday party or afternoon tea. The pansy-covered box adds a summery note.

RECIPE: Light-as-air cake

Preheat the oven to 170°C (325°F/Gas 3). You will need an 18 cm (7 in) ring mould.

RECIPE INGREDIENTS

6 large egg whites

½ teaspoon cream of tartar

¼ teaspoon salt

1 teaspoon (5 ml) vanilla essence

175 g (6 oz) caster sugar

125 g (4 oz) self-raising flour

Few drops edible pink food colouring

18 cm (7 in) ring mould

Makes one 18 cm (7 in) cake

PACKAGING NEEDS

Ruler, string, pencil, scissors, all-purpose glue, tracing or greaseproof paper, craft knife

Round box with lid; the one used here is 23 cm (9 in) in diameter and 10 cm (4 in) deep

2 sheets wrapping paper with floral pattern

Double-sided tape, 5 cm (2 in) wide

At least 60 cm (24 in) thick cord with 2 tasselled ends

Tissue paper, to line box

Small piece of corrugated cardboard, for gift tag

30 cm (12 in) ribbon, 3 mm (⅛ in) wide

1 In a large mixing bowl, using an electric mixer or a hand-held beater, beat the **egg whites** until they are light and foamy. Add the **salt** and **cream of tartar** and continue beating until soft peaks form.

2 Add the **vanilla**, then gradually add the **sugar**, beating between each addition. Continue beating until the mixture becomes stiff.

3 Sift in the **flour** and, using a large metal spoon, fold it into the mixture. Transfer half the mixture to another bowl.

4 Add the **food colouring** to the mixture in one of the bowls and fold it in with the metal spoon. Stop folding as soon as the colour is evenly distributed so that you do not break down the air bubbles. ▶

5 Drop spoonfuls of the plain and pink mixtures alternately into an 18 cm (7 in) ungreased ring mould and level the top with the back of a spoon. (The mould must not be greased otherwise the cake will fall as the fat melts.)

6 Bake the mixture in the preheated oven for 40 to 45 minutes, until a fine skewer inserted in the centre comes out clean. Invert the mould on a rack and leave to cool before turning out the cake. Allow the cake to cool completely, then store it in an airtight container, for up to 3 days, until you are ready to wrap it. ▪▪

GIFTWRAP: Heavenly delight

A deep cardboard box covered with pansy-motif wrapping paper and given chunky cord handles will endure long after the cake has been enjoyed.

1 Measure the side of the box to see how much wrapping paper you need to cover it. The paper strip needs to be as long as the circumference (measure this using string) and as wide as the depth of the box plus 1.5 cm (½ in) on each side for overlap.

3 To cover the top of the lid and base of the box, draw around them on the back of the wrapping paper. Cut out the circles using scissors.

2 Measure the lid in the same way. Using scissors, cut strips of wrapping paper to cover the side of the box and lid.

4 Cover the back of the strips and circles of decorative paper with double-sided tape. Allow the tape to overhang the edges where necessary, then trim to an exact fit with scissors, taking particular care around the edges of the circles.

5 Peel the backing off the tape on the larger strip of wrapping paper. Position the box on its side in the centre of the paper and smooth the paper around the box.

6 Snip into the overlapping edges with scissors to make them easier to stick down. Fold over the edges, first on to the base of the box and then inside the rim.

7 Cover the base of the box with the decorative paper circle after removing the backing from the tape. Cover the side and top of the lid in the same way.

8 To make handles, cut the cord 30 cm (12 in) in from each tassel and knot the free end around the top of the tassel. Glue one handle to each side of the lid, dabbing a little glue on to the free end to prevent it from fraying.

9 Cut a strip of tracing paper to line the inside of the box and a circle to cover the base. Line the box with crumpled tissue paper and put the cake on top. Pull up the tissue paper through the centre of the cake.

10 Cut out some pansies from the giftwrap and glue them on to the lid of the box. (If fresh pansies are in season, you could make a posy instead.) Make a gift tag out of the corrugated cardboard (see page 65, step 6) and glue a cut-out pansy to it. Then tie the tag to one of the handles with the ribbon. ✤

RICH CHRISTMAS FRUITCAKE

BAKED IN A SPHERICAL METAL MOULD, this cake has the appearance of a Victorian-style Christmas plum pudding. A spray of holly or other foliage and berries adds a seasonal note.

RECIPE INGREDIENTS

150g (5oz) plain flour

½ teaspoon salt

1 teaspoon ground cinnamon

¼ teaspoon grated nutmeg

½ teaspoon ground ginger

125g (4oz) unsalted butter, at room temperature

125g (4oz) soft light brown sugar

2 large eggs

150g (5oz) sultanas

150g (5oz) seedless raisins

60g (2oz) dried currants

60g (2oz) blanched almonds, chopped

Grated rind of 1 orange

About 4 tablespoons (60ml) orange juice

1 spherical mould, 12.5cm (5in) in diameter

Makes one 875g (1¾ lb) cake

PACKAGING NEEDS

Greaseproof paper, tape, pencil, scissors, elastic band

Piece of cotton lining material 50 by 50cm (20 by 20in)

Pinking shears (optional)

About 2m (2yd) wire-edged ribbon, 4cm (1½ in) wide

Thin silver-coloured wire

RECIPE: Rich Christmas fruitcake

Preheat the oven to 150°C (300°F/Gas 2). Lightly brush the base and top of a 12.5cm (5in) spherical mould with vegetable oil, then dust them with flour.

1 Sift the **flour**, **salt** and **spices** into a mixing bowl. In another bowl, beat the **butter** and **sugar** with a wooden spoon until the mixture is pale and creamy.

2 Beat the **eggs** one at a time into the creamed butter and sugar, adding about 1 tablespoon of the flour mixture and beating well to prevent the mixture from curdling.

3 Using a large metal spoon, gradually fold in the remaining spiced flour mixture until it is thoroughly incorporated.

4 Stir in the **dried fruits**, chopped **nuts** and **orange rind**. Add just enough of the **orange juice** to give a thick dropping consistency. ▶

5 Spoon the mixture into the base of the prepared mould. Close the mould and bake it in the preheated oven for 2¼ hours, or until a fine skewer inserted through the hole in the top of the mould comes out clean.

6 Leave the cake to cool in the mould, then unclip it and turn out the cake on to a wire rack. When the cake is completely cool, wrap it in foil and store it in an airtight container until you are ready to giftwrap it. ▪▪

GIFTWRAP: Crisp cotton

Wrap the Christmas cake in plain cream cotton and make a statement with the bow. A collection of cakes, all with different ribbons, looks fabulous under the tree.

1 Remove the foil wrapping from the cake. Rewrap the cake in greaseproof paper, keeping the shape as round as possible.

2 Draw and cut sweeping curves from the corners of the cotton. If you wish, cut all around the edges with pinking shears, to prevent fraying and to give a decorative finish.

3 Place the wrapped cake in the centre of the trimmed cloth and draw the sides of the cloth over the top of the cake.

4 Ease the excess material into even folds and hold the cloth tightly in place with the elastic band. Cut a 25 cm (10 in) length of ribbon and tie it around the band to hide it.

5 To make a bow to decorate the parcel, start by forming a 12.5 cm (5 in) loop about halfway along the remaining ribbon.

6 Holding the loop between the thumb and index finger of one hand, cross one end of the ribbon over to form an X-shape at the centre, so making a second loop.

7 Continue crossing the ribbon over at the centre in this way, using first one end of the ribbon and then the other, until you have made three loops on each side.

8 Bind the centre of the bow with the thin wire to secure it, then bind it on to the ribbon around the top of the cake.

9 Adjust the bow to distribute the loops evenly and to conceal the wire. Trim the ribbon ends neatly with scissors. ❋

Note

Instead of using the circular mould, which can also be used to make an ice cream bombe, the mixture can be baked in an earthenware flowerpot. Scrub the flowerpot well and leave it to dry. Then line it with greaseproof paper lightly brushed with oil and dusted with flour.

TEMPLATES

I f you are short of time, or want a more visual aid, here are templates for making some of the more unusual boxes in the book. Each template is shown at exactly half the size of the package; the measurements represent the actual size. Once you have made a box or two, you will be able to adapt the template measurements to suit anything you'd like to package. (To make square or round boxes, see the instructions on pages 6–7 and 8–9, respectively.) ✤

(pages 12–15) *You will need a piece of medium-weight cardboard 25.5 by 43.5 cm (10 by 17 in). Draw the template on to the cardboard, following the given measurements. For a reusable template, transfer the outline on to graph or tracing paper, then draw around it on the cardboard. Alternatively, photocopy the template at 200% to give the exact size (you may need to tape two or more sheets of paper together).*

To make up the box, score all the fold lines, then follow steps 5 and 6 on page 15.

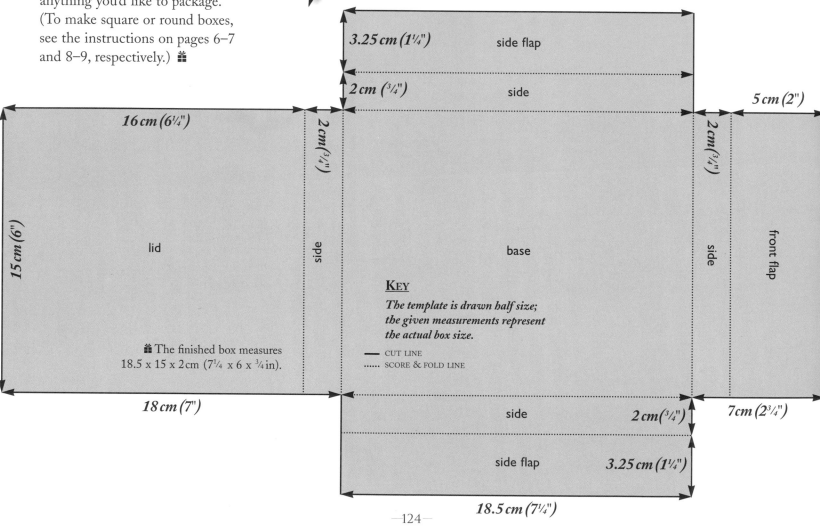

3.25 cm (1¼") — side flap

2 cm (¾") — side

5 cm (2")

16 cm (6¼")

2 cm (¾")

2 cm (¾")

15 cm (6")

lid

side

base

front flap

KEY
The template is drawn half size; the given measurements represent the actual box size.

—— CUT LINE
····· SCORE & FOLD LINE

✤ The finished box measures 18.5 x 15 x 2 cm (7¼ x 6 x ¾ in).

18 cm (7")

side — 2 cm (¾")

7 cm (2¾")

side flap — 3.25 cm (1¼")

18.5 cm (7¼")

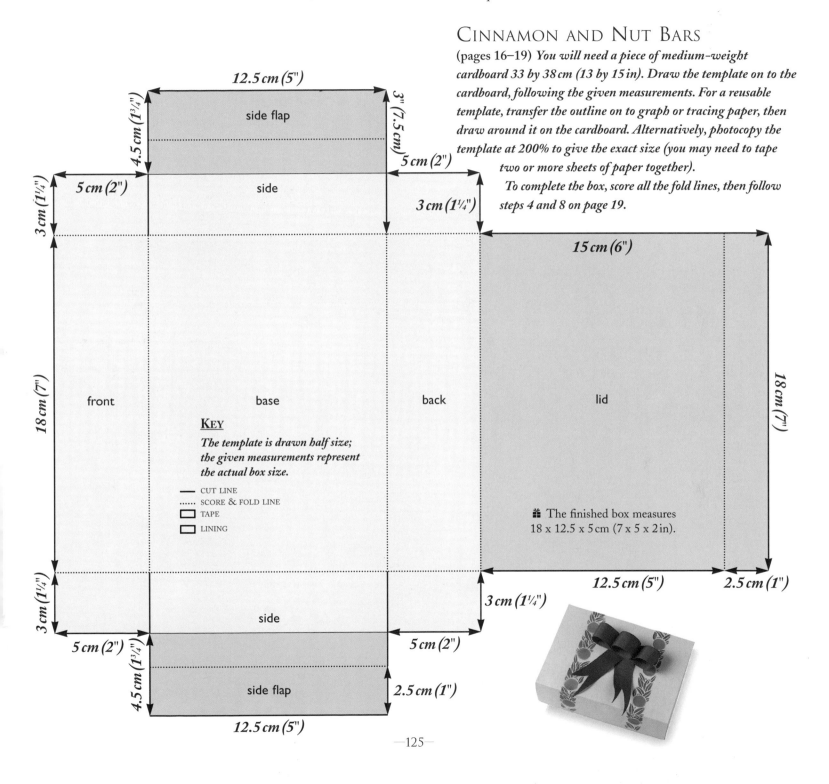

12.5 cm (5")

4.5 cm (1¾")

side flap

3" (7.5 cm)

5 cm (2")

side

5 cm (2")

3 cm (1¼")

3 cm (1¼")

CINNAMON AND NUT BARS

(pages 16–19) *You will need a piece of medium-weight cardboard 33 by 38 cm (13 by 15 in). Draw the template on to the cardboard, following the given measurements. For a reusable template, transfer the outline on to graph or tracing paper, then draw around it on the cardboard. Alternatively, photocopy the template at 200% to give the exact size (you may need to tape two or more sheets of paper together).*

To complete the box, score all the fold lines, then follow steps 4 and 8 on page 19.

15 cm (6")

front

base

back

lid

18 cm (7")

18 cm (7")

KEY
The template is drawn half size; the given measurements represent the actual box size.

—— CUT LINE
········· SCORE & FOLD LINE
▭ TAPE
▭ LINING

✱ The finished box measures 18 x 12.5 x 5 cm (7 x 5 x 2 in).

3 cm (1¼")

side

3 cm (1¼")

5 cm (2")

5 cm (2")

4.5 cm (1¾")

side flap

2.5 cm (1")

12.5 cm (5")

12.5 cm (5")

2.5 cm (1")

SUGAR-FROSTED FRUITS
(pages 82–85) *You will need a piece of medium-weight cardboard 17.3 by 29.8 cm (6¾ by 11⅝ in) for the box and a piece of thinner cardboard 20 by 31 cm (7⅞ by 12¼ in) for the sleeve. Draw the template on to the cardboard, following the given measurements. For a reusable template, transfer the outline on to graph or tracing paper, then draw around it on the cardboard. Alternatively, photocopy the template at 200% to give the exact size (you may need to tape two or more sheets of paper together).*
To make up the box, score along the fold lines, then follow steps 2–4 and 7 on pages 84–85.

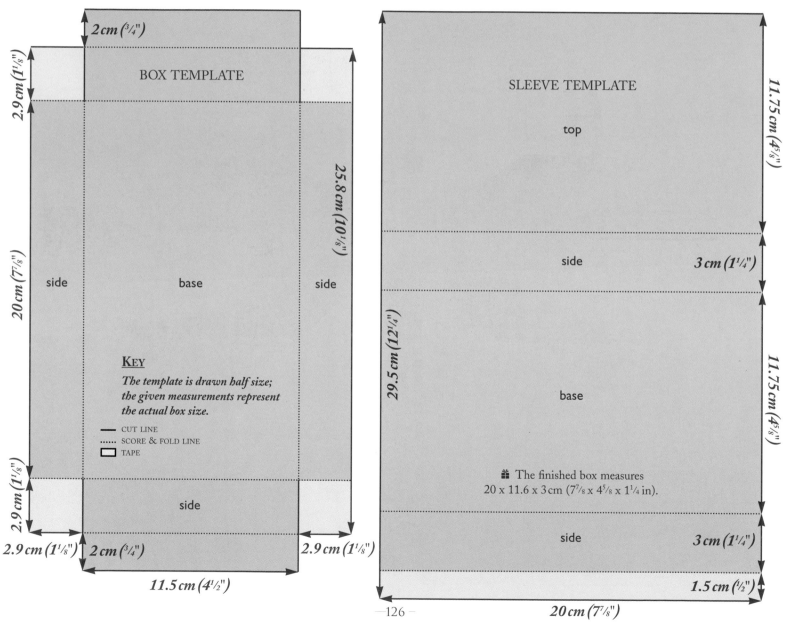

2 cm (¾")

2.9 cm (1⅛")

BOX TEMPLATE

25.8 cm (10⅛")

20 cm (7⅞")

side

base

side

KEY

The template is drawn half size; the given measurements represent the actual box size.

—— CUT LINE
········ SCORE & FOLD LINE
▭ TAPE

2.9 cm (1⅛")

side

2.9 cm (1⅛")   **2 cm (¾")**   **2.9 cm (1⅛")**

11.5 cm (4½")

SLEEVE TEMPLATE

top

11.75 cm (4⅝")

side

3 cm (1¼")

29.5 cm (12¼")

base

11.75 cm (4⅝")

❈ The finished box measures
20 x 11.6 x 3 cm (7⅞ x 4⅝ x 1¼ in).

side

3 cm (1¼")

1.5 cm (½")

20 cm (7⅞")

ACKNOWLEDGEMENTS

The author and publisher are grateful to the following individuals and companies for their assistance in compiling this book.

Margaret Jack for creating the cardboard boxes.

Gary Cross for drawing all the stencil outlines and template artworks.

Christine Ruggles-Brise for devising the paint effects.

ICTC, telephone 01603 488019, for the wire basket on pages 62–65 and the Richard Ginori Impero Rosso dinner plate on pages 100–103.

Offray Ribbons, telephone 01784 247281, for the gossamer, grosgrain, metallic and satin ribbons used for the packages.

Paperchase, telephone 0171 580 8496, for the decorative papers and card used to make the packages.

INDEX